LIVE BEAT 1

WORKBOOK

Rod Fricker

T0346285

Contents

1a I'm OK.

Phrases

1 ⭐ **Complete the phrases with one letter in each gap.**

Gary: Hi, Seth. ¹_H o w_ _a r e_ _y o u_?

Seth: I'm fine, thanks. And you?

Gary: I'm OK. Seth, ²t __ __ __ i __ Amelia.

Seth: Hello, Amelia. ³N __ __ __ t __

m __ __ __ y __ __.

Amelia: Hi.

Gary: Hey, Amelia, Seth, smile!

Amelia/Seth: Oh no! ⁴S __ __ __ i __, Gary.
No photos!

Vocabulary: Numbers 1–100

2 ⭐⭐ **Match the numbers to the words.**

14	fifty
12	forty-one
20	fourteen
15	seventeen
41	thirty-one
50	twelve
17	fifteen
70	seventy
31	twenty

3 ⭐⭐ **Write the numbers in words.**

1 I am (14) _fourteen_.

2 Jenny is (11) _____.

3 My sister is (18) _____.

4 My brother is (23) _____.

5 My teacher is (44) _____.

6 Our town is (100) _____ years old.

Grammar: Verb to be: singular

4 ⭐⭐ **Choose the correct words.**

1 My name **is** / are / am Tom.

2 I **is** / **are** / **am** 14 years old.

3 This **is** / **are** / **am** my sister.

4 **Am** / **Are** / **Is** you a member of this club?

5 **Are** / **Is** / **Am** your name Carole?

6 What **is** / **are** / **am** your name?

5 ⭐⭐ **Make the sentences negative.**

1 I'm fourteen.
I'm not fourteen.

2 He's my friend.
_____

3 Her name is Jane.
_____

4 You're a new member.
_____

5 I'm the new teacher.
_____

6 This is my first time here.
_____

6 ⭐⭐ **Complete the dialogue with the correct form of the verb to be.**

A: ¹_Is_ that Dan?

B: Yes, it ²_____.

A: ³_____ you his sister?

B: Yes, I ⁴_____.

A: How old ⁵_____ he?

B: He ⁶_____ fifteen.

A: ⁷_____ you fifteen?

B: No, I ⁸_____ not. I ⁹_____
thirteen.

A: What ¹⁰_____ your name?

B: Tanya.

7 ★★★ Use the prompts to complete the dialogue.

Sally: Hi. ¹your name/Callum?

Is your name Callum?

Luke: ²no/it/not.

_____

Sally: Oh. ³What/your name?

_____

Luke: ⁴My/name/Luke.

_____

Sally: ⁵How old/you/Luke?

_____

Luke: ⁶I/fifteen.

_____

Sally: ⁷you/a member?

_____

Luke: ⁸no/I/not. ⁹This/my first time here.

_____

Sally: Oh, OK. Nice to meet you, Luke.

Grammar: Singular subject pronouns and possessive adjectives

8 ★ Complete the sentences with the words in capitals.

I/MY

1 *I*'m fourteen.

2 _____ name is Anna.

3 This is _____ brother.

HE/HIS

4 _____ is my boyfriend.

5 _____ name is Ian.

SHE/HER

6 Is that _____ sister?

7 Is _____ a member?

YOU/YOUR

8 Is this _____ phone?

9 How old are _____?

IT/ITS

10 Is that your guitar? No, _____ isn't.

11 My brother is in a band. Cool. What's _____ name?

Grammar summary

Verb to be: *singular*	
Affirmative	**Negative**
I'm (am) fifteen.	**I'm not (am not)** fifteen.
You're (are) new.	You **aren't (are not)** new.
He**'s (is)** my brother.	He **isn't (is not)** my brother.
She**'s (is)** my girlfriend.	She **isn't (is not)** my girlfriend.
It**'s (is)** my phone.	It **isn't (is not)** my phone.
Yes/No Questions	Short answers
Am I your friend?	Yes, you **are**.
	No, you **aren't**.
Are you sixteen?	Yes, I **am**.
	No, I'm not.
Is he your brother?	Yes, he **is**.
	No, he **isn't**.
Is she British?	Yes, she **is**.
	No, she **isn't**.
Is it your photo?	Yes, it **is**.
	No, it **isn't**.

Note

- We usually use contractions in spoken English for affirmative and negative statements.
  *He's fourteen. He **isn't** fourteen.*
- We don't use contractions in affirmative short answers.
  *Yes, **I am**.* NOT ~~Yes, I'm.~~ ✗

Singular subject pronouns and possessive adjectives	
Subject pronouns	Possessive adjectives
I	my
you	your
he	his
she	her
it	its

Note

Subject pronouns
- *I* is always written with a capital letter.

Possessive adjectives
- We use possessive adjectives to talk about something that belongs to someone.
  *Where's **my** mobile phone?*

1b What's your name?

Vocabulary: The alphabet

1 ⭐ **Circle the letter which has a different vowel sound.**

1 ⓒ S M
2 A E H
3 D J G
4 B V W
5 V Q U
6 I Y A
7 K A L
8 X Y F
9 M P N
10 T E I

2 ⭐⭐ **Complete the words with the letters from the box.**

a b c d e f g h i k l m n o
p r s t u v w y

1 M_r_ Smith is my te__cher.
2 __hat's y__ur na__e?
3 __ow __o you s__ell __hat?
4 Is he a mem__er? I don't __now
5 __s Jack yo__r boy__rie__d?
6 How o__d ar__ you? I'm twel__e and my brother is ei__ht.
7 Thi__ is Dave. Hi, Dave. Ni__e to meet __ou.

Vocabulary: Days of the week

3 ⭐ **Complete the days of the week with one letter in each gap.**

1 M _o_ _n_ day
2 T __ __ __ day
3 W __ __ __ __ __ day
4 T __ __ __ __ day
5 F __ __ day
6 S __ __ __ __ day
7 S __ __ day

4 ⭐ Complete with the correct days of the week.

1 _Monday_
My birthday is on Tuesday. That's tomorrow! ☺☺

2 Friday
Great! Tomorrow is _____. ☺

3 _____
Oh no. It's Monday tomorrow. School again. ☹

4 _____
Tomorrow is Thursday. English class. Great!

5 _____
Tomorrow is Wednesday. Great! Drama Club is on Wednesday. It's cool.

6 Thursday
Tomorrow is _____. One more day of school and then the weekend.

7 _____
English class today. My English teacher is cool. And tomorrow is Friday.

Function: Give personal information

5 ⭐ **Match the answers to the correct questions.**

_1–c_

1 What's your first name?   _c_
2 What's your surname?   __
3 How do you spell Mackay?   __
4 What's your address?   __
5 And your postcode?   __
6 What's your home telephone number? __

a) Mackay
b) 0132 324532
c) Cynthia
d) 14 Hope Street, Cambridge
e) M-A-C-K-A-Y
f) CA2 4BB

Use your English: Say hello and goodbye

6 ⭐ **Cross out the response which is wrong.**

1 Hi!
  a) Hi!
  b) Hello.
  c) ~~Bye.~~

2 Hello.
  a) Afternoon.
  b) Goodnight.
  c) Good morning.

3 Good evening.
  a) Evening.
  b) See you later.
  c) Hello.

4 See you later.
  a) Bye.
  b) Hi!
  c) Goodbye.

5 See you.
  a) Goodnight.
  b) Goodbye.
  c) Good morning.

7 ⭐ **Complete the responses with one letter in each gap.**

1 Hi, Jackie.
  H _e_ _l_ _l_ o

2 See you later.
  Yes, g __ __ __ __ __ __ __ t.

3 See you on Friday.
  OK, b __ __.

4 Good morning, Mrs Kemp.
  G __ __ __ m __ __ __ __ __ __ __, Adrian.

5 How are you?
  I'm f __ __ __, thanks.

6 How are things?
  N __ __ b __ __, thanks.

8 ⭐⭐ **Number the conversation in the correct order.**

☐ a) Fine, thanks. And you?

☐ b) Yes, goodbye.

☒ 1 c) Good afternoon, Mrs Davies.

☐ d) Not bad, thanks. See you on Friday.

☐ e) Hello, Ben. How are you?

9 ⭐⭐ **Complete the dialogues with the words from the box.**

> • bad   • Fine   • Good   • Goodnight   • ~~Hi~~
> • How   • on   • See   • thanks   • things

1 A: _Hi_, Leo. _____ are you?
  B: OK, _____. And you?
  A: Not _____.

2 A: _____ morning, Mrs Clarke.
  B: Good morning, Harry. How are _____?
  A: _____, thanks.

3 A: _____ you _____ Monday.
  B: Yes. _____.

1c We're from Poland.

Vocabulary: Countries and nationalities

1 ⭐ **Complete the sentences with the correct country or nationality.**

1 Hi. I'm from the UK. I'm _British_.

2 Hello. I'm from Chile. I'm _____.

3 I'm Portuguese. I'm from _____.

4 I'm from the USA. I'm _____.

5 We're from _____. We're Greek.

6 I'm from Mexico. I'm _____.

7 We're from Italy. We're _____.

8 Hello. I'm from Spain. I'm _____.

Vocabulary: Compass points

2 ⭐⭐ **Look at the arrows. Complete the sentences with compass points.**

1 Buenos Aires is in the
north-east of Argentina.

2 Ciudad Juarez is in the
_____
of Mexico.

3 Vancouver is in the
_____
of Canada.

4 Bourges is in the
_____
of France.

5 Izmir is in the
_____
of Turkey.

6 Bangalore is in the
_____
of India.

Grammar: Verb *to be*: plural

3 ⭐ **Complete the questions and short replies using a plural form of the verb *to be*.**

1 Are you from China?

Yes, _we are_.

2 Are they Irish?

No, _____.

3 Are you Polish?

No, _____.

4 _____ Argentinian?

Yes, they are.

5 Are you from Canada?

Yes, _____.

6 _____ from Japan?

Yes, we are.

4 ⭐⭐ **Complete the dialogue with the correct form of the verb *to be*.**

A: Hello, [1]_Are_ you new members?

B: Yes, we [2]_____.

A: [3]_____ you English?

B: No, we [4]_____. We'[5]_____ from
the USA.

A: Oh, great. Martha and Brad [6]_____
American. They'[7]_____ from Boston.
[8]_____ you from Boston?

B: No, we [9]_____. We'[10]_____ from
Los Angeles.

A: Los Angeles! Wow. That's cool. Welcome to
the club.

5 ★★★ **Complete the questions and answers.**

1 What/your names?

Our names/Gene and Sami

What are your names?
Our names are Gene and Sami.

2 How old/Chris and Debbie?

They/fifteen.

_____

_____

3 you/American?

No/we/not. We/Australian

_____

_____

4 Hi. We/new members. We/Tanya and Sophie.

Hi. What/surnames?

_____

_____

Grammar: Subject pronouns: *we, you, they*

6 ★ **Rewrite the sentences with a plural subject pronoun.**

1 I am 14. My friend is fourteen. *We are fourteen*.

2 You're Polish. You're Polish.

_____

3 He's German. She's German.

_____

4 She's my sister. She's my sister.

_____

5 I'm from France. You're from France.

_____

6 He's from China. She's from China. He's from

China. _____

Grammar summary

Verb *to be*: plural	
Affirmative	**Negative**
We**'re (are)** fourteen years old.	We **aren't (are not)** fourteen years old.
You**'re (are)** Canadian.	You **aren't (are not)** Canadian.
They**'re (are)** brothers.	They **aren't (are not)** brothers.
Yes/No Questions	**Short answers**
Are we in the north of Poland?	Yes, we/you **are**. No, we/you **aren't**.
Are you Italian?	Yes, we **are**. No, we **aren't**.
Are they from France?	Yes, they **are**. No, they **aren't**.

Note

- We use *are* for all plural forms of the verb *to be*.
- We usually use contractions in spoken English for affirmative and negative statements. *We**'re** fourteen. You**'re** fourteen. They **aren't** fourteen.*
- We don't use contractions in affirmative short answers. **Yes, we are**. NOT ~~Yes, We're.~~ ✗

Plural subject pronouns: *we, you, they*
we
you
they

Note

Subject pronouns

- In English, the subject pronoun *you* is both singular and plural.

1 Language round-up

1 Complete the dialogues with the correct subject pronoun or possessive adjective.

A: Hi Debbie. Is that ¹_your_ phone?

B: No, ²_____ isn't. This is ³_____ phone, here. Where's Mike?

A: ⁴_____'s at school. Why?

B: That's ⁵_____ phone.

A: Hi, ⁶_____ name's Laura and this is my sister. ⁷_____ name is Sandy. ⁸_____'s fourteen years old. ⁹_____ are Canadian.

B: Hi, Laura. Hi, Sandy. Beth and Simon are Canadian. ¹⁰_____ are from Toronto. Are you from Toronto?

A: No, ¹¹_____ aren't. ¹²_____'re from Vancouver.

.../11

2 Complete the dialogue with the phrases from the box.

• are from • Are you • Are your
• His name • Her parents are • I'm not
• is English • ~~is my~~ • south-east

Sara: Hi, Becky.

Becky: Hello, Sara. This ¹_is my_ brother. ²_____ is Sam.

Sara: Nice to meet you, Sam.

Sam: And you. ³_____ American, Sara?

Sara: No, ⁴_____. I'm from Canada. My family ⁵_____ Toronto. It's a big city in the ⁶_____ of Canada.

Sam: ⁷_____ parents Canadian?

Sara: My dad's Canadian, but my mum ⁸_____. ⁹_____ from London.

.../8

3 Complete the words with one letter in each gap.

Five countries:

1 I _n_ d _i_ _a_   4 __ h __ l __

2 S __ __ i __   5 __ t __ l __

3 __ h __ n __

Five nationalities:

6 G __ __ m __ __   9 I __ __ s __

7 __ r __ t __ __ h   10 F __ __ n __ __

8 __ r __ __ k

Five numbers:

11 e __ __ v __ __   14 f __ __ t __ __ n

12 __ __ g __ t   15 __ o __ __ y

13 __ w __ __ v __

.../14

4 Read the text and choose the correct answers.

Hi,

¹_My_ name is Jeanne. I am fifteen. This is my photo. I'm with my boyfriend. ²_____ name is Ed. We ³_____ from Arundel. ⁴_____ a beautiful town in the south of England.

My parents ⁵_____ teachers. My dad is an English teacher and my mum is a French teacher. ⁶_____ parents are French. ⁷_____ are from Lille. Lille is a city in the north of ⁸_____.

1 a) I	b) My	c) Her
2 a) My	b) Her	c) His
3 a) is	b) am	c) are
4 a) He's	b) We're	c) It's
5 a) they	b) are	c) is
6 a) Her	b) His	c) My
7 a) We	b) They	c) You
8 a) French	b) France	c) the centre

.../7

🔊 2 **LISTEN AND CHECK YOUR SCORE**

Total	.../40

1 Skills practice

SKILLS FOCUS: **READING** AND **WRITING**

Read

1 Read about three towns in the UK and label the photos with the correct names.

A

B

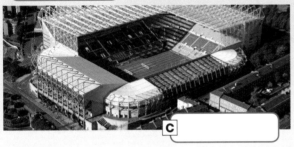

C

1 Newcastle is a fantastic city in the north-east of England. It's famous for its football team, Newcastle United. Newcastle University and Northumbria University are both in the city of Newcastle.

2 Windsor is a town in the south-east of England. It's a very beautiful town. It's famous for its castle. The castle is very big.

3 Tenby is in the south-west of Wales. It's a fantastic town. It's famous for its beautiful beaches.

2 Read the text again and complete the table.

	Where it is	Famous for
Newcastle	1 *north-east England*	2
Windsor	3	4
Tenby	5	6

3 Now complete the map with the three towns in the correct places.

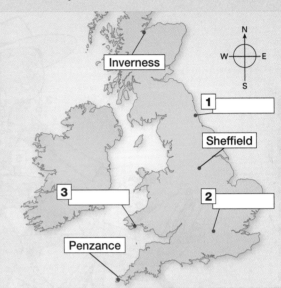

Inverness

1

Sheffield

3

2

Penzance

Write

4 Rewrite the letter using full stops, apostrophes and capital letters.

> hi,
> our names are steven and alison i am fifteen and alison is thirteen shes my sister. were from colchester. it's a town in the east of england our dad is from london. our mum is greek. we speak english and greek our grandparents are in thessaloniki. its a city in the north of greece.

Hi,
Our names are Steven and Alison. …

5 Now use the information to write a new letter.

Writer's name:	Kinga Jenson
Age:	fifteen
Town:	Southampton
Where:	South of England
Father:	British – from Winchester
Mother:	Polish – from Torun
Languages:	Polish and English
Grandparents:	Torun – city, centre of Poland

Hi,
My name's Kinga Jenson. …

2a What's that?

Vocabulary: Everyday things

1 ⭐ Look at the picture and complete the names of the objects (1–12).

1 h<u>at</u>   7 p_____
2 r_____   8 s_____
3 e_____   9 a_____
4 d_____   10 b_____
5 w_____   11 b_____
6 ID c_____   12 t_____

Grammar: Indefinite article: a/an

2 ⭐ Tick the sentences which are correct. Correct the sentences which are wrong.

1 It's a apple. ✗
  It's an apple.

2 It's a book.
  _____

3 It's a diary.
  _____

4 It's an sandwich.
  _____

5 It's a earring.
  _____

6 It's an exercise book.
  _____

7 It's an hat.
  _____

8 It's a MP3 player.
  _____

9 It's a photo.
  _____

10 It's an watch.
  _____

3 ⭐⭐ Choose the answers which are not correct.

1 It's an ___.
  a) earring   b) apple
  ⓒ earrings

2 It's a ___.
  a) book   b) exercise book
  c) diary

3 They're ___.
  a) keys   b) a sandwich
  c) bikes

4 It's an ___.
  a) DVD   b) MP3 player
  c) ID card

5 They're ___.
  a) a trainer   b) trainers
  c) watches

6 It's a ___.
  a) photo   b) key
  c) sandwiches

Phrases

4 ⭐ Complete the replies.

1 A: Hey! They're my sandwiches.
  B: Oh, s<u>orry</u>.

2 A: Where's my MP3 player?
     Where is it?
  B: C_____ d_____!

3 A: Oh, are they your cheese
     sandwiches?
  B: Yes. H_____
     y_____.
  A: Thanks.

4 A: What's David's mobile number?
     My diary's at home.
  B: His number is 012557483.
  A: Oh great. W_____
     d_____.

Grammar: Regular noun plurals

5 ⭐ **Look at the pictures and complete the sentences.**

1 They're _keys_.

2 They're _____.

3 They're _____.

4 They're _____.

5 They're _____.

6 They're _____.

Grammar: Demonstrative pronouns: *this, that, these, those*

6 ⭐ **Complete the dialogue with *this, that, these* or *those*.**

A: Hi, Simon. ¹_These_ are my photos from Greece.

B: Oh great!

A: ²_____ one is me and my sister on the beach. And ³_____ two photos are of a castle in the town. Oh, and ... what's wrong?

B: Sorry. Is ⁴_____ your camera?

A: No, ⁵_____ isn't my camera, but ⁶_____ are my keys.

B: And ⁷_____ is my bag there.

A: Are ⁸_____ your sandwiches?

B: Yes, they are. Oh no.

Grammar summary

Indefinite article: *a/an*

It's **a** bike.
It isn't **a** DVD.
Is it **a** camera?
It's **an** MP3 player.
It isn't **an** earring.
Is it **an** exercise book?

Note

- We use ***a/an*** before a noun when we talk about one person or thing.
- We use *a* before a consonant sound.
- We use *an* before a vowel sound (*a, e, i, o, u*).
- The sound of the first letter of the noun after *a/an* is important:
  An MP3 player (/em/)

Regular noun plurals

book	book**s**
key	key**s**
diary	diar**ies**
sandwich	sandwich**es**
watch	watch**es**

Note

- To make most nouns plural, we add *-s*.

Spelling rules

- When a noun ends in a vowel + *-y*, we add *-s*.
  day – days
- When a noun ends in a consonant + *-y*, the *-y* changes to *-i* and we add *-es*.
  diary – diaries
- When a noun ends in *-ch*, *-sh*, *-ss*, *-s* or *-x*, we add *-es*.
  address – addresses

Demonstrative pronouns

| **This** photo | **These** photos |
| **That** hat | **Those** hats |

Note

- We use *this* and *these* to talk about things or people that are near to us.
- We use *that* and *those* for things or people that are not near to us.

Vocabulary: Clothes

1 ⭐ **Label the pictures with the words from the box.**

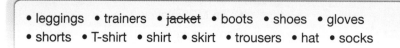

> • leggings • trainers • ~~jacket~~ • boots • shoes • gloves
> • shorts • T-shirt • shirt • skirt • trousers • hat • socks

A _jacket_

B _____

C _____

D _____

E _____

F _____

G _____

H _____

I _____

J _____

K _____

L _____

M _____

Grammar: Genitive 's (singular) and s' (plural)

2 ⭐ **Choose the correct options.**

1 My brother's guitar.

  a) One brother   b) Two or more brothers

2 My friends' phones.

  a) One friend   b) Two or more friends

3 My parents' car.

  a) One parent   b) Two parents

4 My teacher's books.

  a) One teacher   b) Two or more teachers

5 My dogs' friends.

  a) One dog   b) Two or more dogs

6 My teachers' clothes.

  a) One teacher   b) Two or more teachers

3 ⭐⭐ **Underline the genitive 's/s'. Don't underline 's when it means _is_.**

1 My name's Glenn. This is my <u>brother's</u> book.

2 My friend's phone is cool. It's a smartphone.

3 My parents' car is red. That's my parents' car in the photo.

4 This is my friend Jacek. Jacek's Polish. Jacek's parents are from Gdansk.

5 Maria's fifteen. She's a singer. Maria's mother is a singer. Her father's a teacher.

6 My jacket's black. My sister's jacket's red.

7 This DVD's great. It's my favourite.

8 My cousins' dog's very friendly.

4 ★★★ **Make sentences. Use a genitive 's/s' in each sentence.**

1 This/Tom/book

This is Tom's book.

2 These/my sisters/shoes. The red shoes are Alison's and the blue shoes are Carole's.

_____

3 Those/not/my mum/keys

_____

4 These/my parents/watches

_____

5 That/my friend/bike

_____

6 This/Helen/MP3

_____

Grammar: Possessive adjectives: *our, your, their*

5 ★ **Change the subject pronouns into the correct possessive adjective.**

Cathy: What are ¹*your* (you) names?

Girls: ² _____ (We) names are Elaine and Nicola.

Stuart: Are ³ _____ (they) names Emma and Natalie?

Cathy: No. ⁴ _____ (They) names are Elaine and Nicola.

Stuart: Hi, Elaine. Hi, Nicola. Are you English?

Girls: ⁵ _____ (We) mother is English, but ⁶ _____ (we) father is French.

Stuart: Is ⁷ _____ (you) father from Paris?

Girls: No, he isn't. He's from Rouen.

Vocabulary: Colours

6 ★ **Complete the colours.**

1 Blue and yellow = g*reen*

2 Red and blue = p_____

3 Black and white = g_____

4 Red and white = p_____

5 Red and yellow = o_____

6 Red and green = b_____

7 Brown and white and yellow = b_____

Grammar summary

Genitive 's (singular) and s' (plural)

My brother**'s** guitar.
Harry**'s** books.
My parent**s'** friends.
The teacher**s'** cars.

Note

Use

• We use 's and s' to talk about possession.

Form

• We use 's after a singular noun.
• We use s' after a plural noun.
• When a singular noun ends in -s, we don't usually add an extra -s.
  Charles – Charles' trainers

Common mistake

~~This is the shirt of my brother.~~ ✗
This is my **brother's** shirt. ✓

Possessive adjectives: *our, your, their*

our
your
their

Note

• We use possessive adjectives before nouns to talk about something that belongs to someone.
  *This is **our** house.*
• The possessive adjective *your* is both singular and plural.

2c How much is that?

Vocabulary: Fast food and drink

1 ⭐ **Complete the foods.**

1 b<u>urger</u>

2 h _____
  d _____

3 c _____

4 c _____

5 c _____

6 c _____

7 h _____
  c _____

8 m _____
  w _____

9 i _____
  c _____

10 t _____

Vocabulary: Money

2 ⭐ **Look at the menu and complete the sentences.**

menu

BURGERS   £1·75p
COLA   80p
HOT DOGS £1·50p
JUICE
    orange 90p
    apple   70p
SANDWICHES
    chicken £1·80p
    cheese £1·60p
COFFEE   £1·20p

1 A cheese sandwich is <u>one pound sixty</u>.

2 A chicken sandwich is

_____.

3 A burger is _____.

4 A cola is _____.

5 An orange juice is _____.

6 A coffee is _____.

Grammar: Can (request)

3 ⭐ **Rewrite the sentences using 'Can I/we have ... , please?'.**

1 I want a burger and chips.

   <u>Can I have a burger and chips, please?</u>

2 I want a cheese sandwich and a cola.

   _____

3 We want two mineral waters.

   _____

4 We want two hot dogs.

   _____

5 A packet of crisps and a coffee.

   _____

6 Two ice creams.

   _____

Use your English: Order food and drink

4 ⭐ **Read the sentences. Who says them? Write C (Customer) or A (Assistant).**

1 Can I have a sandwich, please?   <u>C</u>

2 That's £3.20 altogether.   —

3 Anything else?   —

4 How much is a cola?   —

5 Chicken or cheese?   —

6 OK, can I have a cheese
  sandwich and a cola, please?   —

7 £1.20.   —

8 Cheese, please.   —

5 ⭐⭐ **Complete the conversation with words from the box.**

> • altogether • Can • dogs • else • Here
> • How • ~~much~~ • pence • portion • pound

Customer: Good morning. How ¹ <u>much</u> are chips?

Assistant: Chips are ninety-five ²_____.

Customer: ³_____ I have a ⁴_____ of chips, please?

Assistant: Anything ⁵_____?

Customer: ⁶_____ much are hot ⁷_____ ?

Assistant: One ⁸_____ fifty.

Customer: OK, chips and a hot dog, please.

Assistant: That's two pounds forty-five pence ⁹_____, thank you. ¹⁰_____ you are.

Customer: Thank you.

Grammar summary

Can (request)

Can I have a burger, please?
Can I have a coffee, please?
Can we have two portions of chips, please?
Can we have two hot dogs, please?

Note

- To make a request, we use *Can* + subject + infinitive of the verb without *to*.
  Can we **have** a drink, please?

Common mistake

~~Can we to have a burger?~~ ✗
Can we **have** a burger. ✓
~~I can have a packet of crisps?~~ ✗
Can I **have** a packet of crisps? ✓

2 Language round-up

1 Make sentences.

1 Can/have/burger/?

Can I have a burger, please?

2 Can/have/two/sandwich?

_____

3 these/your/diary?

_____

4 Can/have/apple juice?

_____

5 Those/my sister/earrings

_____

6 That/cool/T-shirt

_____

.../10

2 Complete the dialogue with the words from the box.

• ~~these~~ • Here • our • altogether • Your
• pound • their • much • dog • that
• expensive

Will:	Here's the food. Rob, Charles, are ¹*these* your burgers?
Rob:	No, they aren't.
Cathy, Becky:	They're ² _____ burgers.
Will:	Oh, sorry.
Cathy:	How ³ _____ are burgers here?
Will:	They're one ⁴ _____ forty-five.
Cathy:	Really? That's ⁵ _____ . They're 90p at Star Burger.
Will:	But they're good here. Sam, here's your hot ⁶ _____ and your chips. £1.40 plus 80p, that's £2.20 ⁷ _____ .
Sam:	OK. ⁸ _____ you are.
Will:	Thanks. Where are Gina and Josie? These are ⁹ _____ sandwiches.
Sam:	There they are. They're in ¹⁰ _____ shop. Gina, Josie! ¹¹ _____ food is here.
Gina:	OK, thanks.

.../10

3 Choose the correct options.

1 Our / **Their** names are Jenny and Stephanie.

2 **These** / **This** blog is about our favourite things.

3 **Jennys'** / **Jenny's** favourite sport is tennis.

4 Our favourite shop is Crazy Town. **Their** / **They** clothes are cool.

5 My **parents** / **parents'** favourite shop is LookRight. It's boring!

6 My favourite possession is my MP3 **player** / **phone**.

7 **That** / **These** are my favourite earrings.

8 My favourite food is ice cream and a mineral **drink** / **water**.

9 My favourite fast food is **an** / **a** hot dog.

10 The **hot** / **portion** chocolate at Bob's Burgers is fantastic.

.../9

4 Rearrange the letters to make words and put them in the correct column.

• ~~atjcek~~ • hicsp • urbreg • egbie
• uepprl • rstoesur • ahisnwdc • riesvl
• senilggg • hieccnk • lolwye • solveg

Clothes	Food	Colours
jacket		
_____	_____	_____
_____	_____	_____
_____	_____	_____
_____	_____	

.../11

🎧 3 LISTEN AND CHECK YOUR SCORE

Total	.../40

2 Skills practice

SKILLS FOCUS: READING, LISTENING AND WRITING

Read

1 Read the dialogue quickly. Tick the things the boys talk about.

1 flowers	✓	6 bracelet	☐
2 earrings	☐	7 game	☐
3 trainers	☐	8 gloves	☐
4 DVD	☐	9 watch	☐
5 mobile phone	☐		

Mark: It's my mother's birthday on Saturday, my father's birthday on Sunday, my girlfriend's birthday on Monday, my brother's birthday on Tuesday and my sister's birthday on Wednesday!

Will: Oh, dear. How about flowers for your mother?

Mark: I'm not sure.

Will: How about these earrings?

Mark: Oh yes, good idea. How much are they?

Will: They're £5.

Mark: Great.

Will: And this DVD for your dad. It isn't expensive. It's only £2.99.

Mark: OK. Now. My girlfriend.

Will: How about flowers and this bracelet?

Mark: The bracelet's £12. That's expensive. The flowers are OK. They're £4.

Will: So, flowers for your girlfriend.

Mark: Yes, and this game for my brother. It's £1.99. What about my sister?

Will: I know. Gloves. These gloves are cool. They're £3.

Mark: How much is that altogether?

Will: Er ... £16.98.

Mark: Great ... er, can I borrow £5?

2 Read the dialogue again and complete the table.

Who the present is for	Present	How much it is
His mother	1 *earrings*	2 _____
His father	3 _____	4 _____
His girlfriend	5 _____	6 _____
His brother	7 _____	8 _____
His sister	9 _____	10 *£3*

Listen

3 🎧 **4 Listen to six conversations. Choose the items they talk about and the prices.**

1 a) Skirts / Shirts   b) £6.99 / £6.19

2 a) **Trainers / Trousers**   b) **£12 / £20**

3 a) **Boots / Shoes**   b) **£15.50 / £16.50**

4 a) **Cheese / Chicken sandwich**
   b) **£1.80 / £1.90**

5 a) **Chips / Crisps**   b) **95p / 59p**

6 a) **Hot dog / chocolate** b) **£1.60 / £1.50**

Write

4 Complete the conversation with the words and phrases from the box.

- Can I help you?   • How about these
- How about this • How much is it?
- How much are they?

Shop assistant: Hello. ¹*Can I help you?*

You: Yes, please. I'd like to buy a present for my grandmother. It's her birthday.

Shop assistant: ² _____ gloves?

You: They're very nice. ³ _____

Shop assistant: They're £10.

You: Oh, they're expensive.

Shop assistant: ⁴ _____ hat?

You: ⁵ _____

Shop assistant: It's only £5.

You: That's great!

3a There's a garden!

Vocabulary: Rooms, parts of a house and fittings

1 ⭐ **Label the rooms.**

A *bathroom*

B _____

C _____

D _____

2 ⭐⭐ **Match the words to the objects in the pictures.**

bath – 1

- ~~bath~~ • washing machine • window
- door • cooker • sink • wall
- toilet • fridge • washbasin • floor

Grammar: *There is, there are:* affirmative, negative, questions

3 ⭐ **Complete the sentences with the correct form of *there is* or *there are*.**

1 *There is* a kitchen. ✓
2 _____ a dining room. ✗
3 _____ big windows. ✓
4 _____ a dishwasher?
5 _____ two bathrooms. ✗
6 _____ three bedrooms?

4 ⭐⭐ **Complete the dialogue. Use the prompts and the correct form of *there is* or *there are*.**

Mike: This is our new house.

Callum: ¹*Is there a dining room?*
there/dining room

Mike: ² _____ ✓

Callum: ³ _____
there/dishwasher

Mike: ⁴ _____ ✗

Callum: ⁵ _____
there/two bathrooms

Mike: ⁶ _____ ✗
⁷only one – but very big
_____

Callum: ⁸ _____
there/shower or bath

Mike: ⁹ _____ ✓
shower and bath

Callum: ¹⁰ _____
there/garage

Mike: ¹¹ _____ ✓
and/garden

Callum: Where's your bedroom?

Mike: Upstairs. Come on.

5 ★★ Complete the questions and answers about the picture.

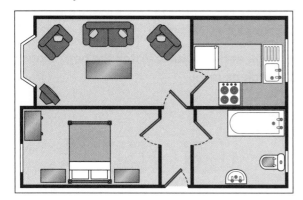

1 Is there a cooker in the kitchen?

   Yes, there is.

2 _____ any flowers in the bathroom?

   _____

3 _____ a TV in the bedroom?

   _____

4 _____ any chairs in the living room?

   _____

5 _____ a toilet in the bathroom?

   _____

Grammar: Definite article: *the*

6 ★ Complete the dialogues with *a/an* and *the*.

1 A: There's <u>an</u> apple in my bag.

   B: What colour is <u>the</u> apple?

2 A: This is _____ kitchen.

   B: Is there _____ dishwasher in here?

3 A: Can I have _____ drink?

   B: No. _____ drinks here are expensive.

7 ★★ Complete the text with *a*, *an* or *the*.

In my house there's ¹<u>a</u> kitchen and ²_____ living room downstairs. There isn't ³_____ dining room. In ⁴_____ kitchen, there's ⁵_____ cooker, ⁶_____ fridge and ⁷_____ dishwasher. ⁸_____ dishwasher is new. Upstairs, there's ⁹_____ bathroom and there are three bedrooms. There's ¹⁰_____ garage and ¹¹_____ big garden. In ¹²_____ garage, there's ¹³_____ car and ¹⁴_____ bike.

Grammar summary

There is, there are

Affirmative	Negative
There's a bike in the hall.	**There isn't** a bike in the hall.
There's an apple in the kitchen.	**There isn't** an apple in the kitchen.
There are three bedrooms.	**There aren't** three bedrooms.
There are green walls.	**There aren't** green walls.
Questions	Short answers
Is there a shower in the bathroom?	Yes, **there is.**/No, **there isn't.**
Are there two bathrooms?	Yes, **there are.**/No, **there aren't.**

Note

Use
- We use *there is (there's)* with singular people or things and *there are* with plurals.
  There's a kitchen.
  There are three bedrooms.

Common mistakes
~~Is a sink in the kitchen?~~ ✗
Is there a sink in the kitchen? ✓

Definite article: *the*

There's a window in **the** bathroom. **The** window is small.

Note
- We use *the* with a singular or plural noun when we know which thing we are talking about.
  It's in **the** kitchen. (There is only one kitchen.)
  There's a window in the living room. **The** window is very big. (We know which window.)
- We can't use *the* with *there is/there are*.
  There is a kitchen. (There is only one kitchen, but we can't use *the*.)

Common mistakes
~~There's a cooker in a kitchen.~~ ✗
There's a cooker in the kitchen. ✓

3b It's in the bin.

Vocabulary: Furniture

1 ⭐ **Complete the furniture words with one letter in each space.**

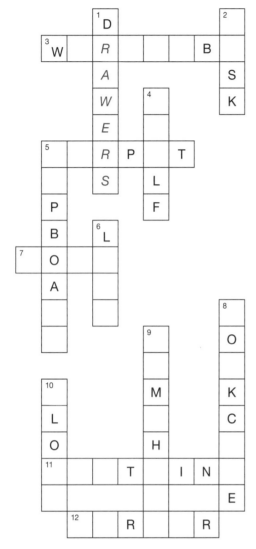

Phrases

2 ⭐ **Choose the correct words.**

1 **A:** Oh no!

B: What's the **mind** / **matter** / **need**?

A: My phone isn't in my bag.

2 **A:** This is my bedroom.

B: What a **mess** / **lot** / **great**!

3 **A:** Where's your bag?

B: **Away** / **Over** / **Under** there. Next to the desk.

4 **A:** Hey! That's my sandwich.

B: It's great! My favourite.

A: It's not **my** / **ready** / **funny**. I'm hungry.

Grammar: Prepositions of place: *in, on, under, behind, in front of, next to*

3 ⭐ **Look at the picture. Match the beginnings (1–8) to the endings (a–h).**

1 The clocks   a) is in front of the bookcase.

2 The table   b) is next to the desk.

3 The lamp   c) are on the shelf.

4 The wastepaper bin d) are on the walls.

5 The armchair   e) is on the desk.

6 The plants   f) is next to the windows.

7 The mirror   g) is under one of the clocks.

8 The desk   h) is on the carpet.

4 ⭐⭐ **Look at the picture again and write sentences.**

1 carpet/floor

The carpet is on the floor.

2 bookcase/armchair

The bookcase _____.

3 lamp/computer

The lamp _____.

4 computer/desk

The computer _____.

5 chair/desk

The chair _____.

6 paper/wastepaper bin

The paper _____.

7 table/sofa

The table _____.

8 carpet/sofa

The carpet _____.

Use your English: Make and respond to requests

5 ⭐ **Complete the dialogues with words from the box.**

> • sorry • Can • of • it • here • your
> • hat • need • course • borrow

1 A: Can I borrow your MP3 player?

   B: Yes, _of_ course.

2 A: _____ I borrow your watch?

   B: No, I'm _____, I need _____.

3 A: Can I borrow your _____?

   B: Yes, OK, _____ you are.

4 A: Can I _____ your gloves?

   B: I'm sorry, I _____ them.

5 A: Can I borrow _____ pen?

   B: Yes, of _____.

6 ⭐⭐ **Use the prompts to make conversations.**

1 A: borrow/phone?

   B: sorry/need

   A: Can I borrow your phone?

   B: I'm sorry. I need it.

2 A: borrow/bike?

   B: Yes/course

   _____

   _____

3 A: borrow/guitar?

   B: Yes/here

   _____

   _____

4 A: borrow/camera

   B: sorry/need

   _____

   _____

Grammar summary

Prepositions of place: *in, on, under, behind, in front of, next to*

There's a sofa **in** the living room.
There's a pen **on** the table.
The wastepaper bin is **under** the desk.
Your book is **behind** the wardrobe.
The desk is **in front of** the window.
The fridge is **next to** the sink.

Note

- We use prepositions of place to say where somebody or something is.

Form

- We always follow *next* with *to*. We can't use it on its own.
- We always follow *in front* with *of*.

Common mistakes

~~The bed is next the wall.~~ ✗
The bed is **next to** the wall. ✓
~~The television is in front the bookcase.~~ ✗
The television is **in front of** the bookcase. ✓

3c Is there any food?

Vocabulary: Food

1 ★★ **Label the picture.**

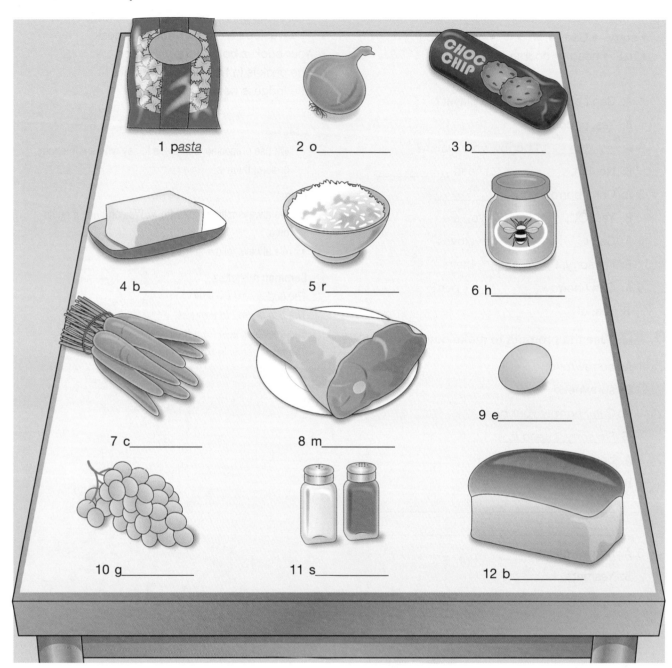

1 p*asta*

2 o_____

3 b_____

4 b_____

5 r_____

6 h_____

7 c_____

8 m_____

9 e_____

10 g_____

11 s_____

12 b_____

Grammar: Countable and uncountable nouns with *some* and *any*

2 ★ **Underline the countable words.**

1 <u>apple</u>, <u>banana</u>, <u>biscuit</u>, bread

2 butter, carrot, cheese, chicken

3 chips, egg, pasta, grape

4 honey, meat, onion, orange

5 pepper, potato, rice, salt

6 sugar, tomato, burger, water

3 ★ **Complete the sentences with *is*, *are*, *isn't* or *aren't*.**

1 There *is* some butter.

2 There _____ any meat.

3 _____ there any pasta?

4 _____ there any eggs?

5 There _____ some potatoes.

6 There _____ some bread.

7 There _____ any grapes.

4 ★★ **Look at the list. Complete the questions and short answers with the correct form of *is/are* and *any*.**

> cheese ✗   carrots ✗
> tomatoes ✓   bananas ✗
> rice ✓   sugar ✗

1 *Is* there *any* cheese?

No, there *isn't*.

2 _____ there _____ rice?

Yes, there _____.

3 _____ there _____ bananas?

No, there _____.

4 _____ there _____ tomatoes?

Yes, there _____.

5 _____ there _____ carrots?

No, there _____.

6 _____ there _____ sugar?

No, there _____.

5 ★★★ **Complete the dialogue using the prompts and *some* or *any*.**

Emily: ¹*Is there any pasta?* (there/pasta)?

Janet: ²_____ (No/not).

³_____ (There/rice and there/potatoes).

Emily: Great. ⁴_____ (there/onions)?

Jane: ⁵_____ (No/not).

⁶_____ (There/ carrots).

Emily: Oh no. ⁷_____ (There/not/meat).

Jane: That's OK. ⁸_____ (There/cheese).

Emily: Potatoes, rice, carrots and cheese?

Jane: Yes. What's the matter?

Emily: Well ... ⁹_____ (there/bread)?

Jane: No, ¹⁰_____ (but/ biscuits).

Emily: Oh great!

Grammar summary

Countable and uncountable nouns with *some* and *any*

Countable nouns

Affirmative	Negative
There is an apple.	There isn't a dishwasher.
There are **some** eggs.	There aren't **any** oranges.

Questions and short answers

Singular	Plural
Is there a garden?	Are there **any** onions?
Yes, there is.	Yes, there are.
No, there isn't.	No, there aren't.

Uncountable nouns

Affirmative	Negative
There is **some** bread.	There isn't **any** sugar.
There is **some** butter.	There isn't **any** salt.

Yes/No Questions and short answers.	
Is there **any** pepper?	
Yes, there is. No, there isn't.	

Note

- Countable nouns can be singular or plural. We can count them and use *a/an* or numbers with them.
- Uncountable nouns:
  - are usually not plural
  - cannot be counted
  - don't have numbers or *a/an* with them
  - take the singular form of the verb *to be* (*is*).
- We use *some* with *there is* in affirmative sentences with uncountable nouns. We use *some* with *there are* in affirmative sentences with plural countable nouns when we don't give an exact number.
  *There is **some** salt.*
  *There are **some** grapes.*
- We use *any* with *there is* in negative sentences and questions with uncountable nouns. We use *any* with *there are* in negative sentences and questions with plural countable nouns.
  *There isn't **any** pepper.*
  *Is there **any** bread?*
  *There **aren't** any apples.*
  ***Are** there any bananas?*

Common mistake

~~There isn't some rice.~~ ✗

There isn't **any** rice. ✓

- We don't use *some* or *any* with singular, countable nouns.

Common mistakes

~~There isn't any dining room.~~ ✗

There isn't **a** dining room. ✓

~~Is there any fridge?~~ ✗

Is there **a** fridge? ✓

3 Language round-up

1 Look at the pictures and choose the correct options.

1 There **is** / **are** some bread **on** / **in** the table.

2 There **is** / **are** some potatoes **in front of** / **next to** the bread.

3 There aren't **some** / **any** bananas on **a** / **the** table.

4 There is **the** / **a** bookcase in the picture.

5 There is some paper **on** / **in** the bookcase.

6 There is **a** / **the** book **under** / **in** the bookcase.

7 In this picture, there is **a** / **the** chair, **a** / **the** wastepaper bin and **a** / **the** desk.

8 The chair is **behind** / **in front of the** / **a** desk.

9 **The** / **some** wastepaper bin is **under** / **in** the desk.

10 There is **a** / **the** plant **behind** / **in front of** the curtains.

11 There are **some** / **any** posters **on** / **in** the wall.

...../19

2 Complete the text with one word in each space.

In my aunt's house, ¹*there* are three bedrooms, two bathrooms, a kitchen, a living room and a dining ²_____. In ³_____ living room, there's a TV, a sofa and three armchairs. The sofa is ⁴_____ front of a bookcase. There are ⁵_____ lot of great books in the bookcase, but there aren't ⁶_____ DVDs.

...../10

3 Complete the words to find where Ben's phone is.

	¹B	U	T	T	E	R	
		²					
	³						
		⁴					
⁵							
		⁶					
		⁷					
			⁸				
	⁹						
		¹⁰					
	¹¹						
¹²							

1 I'd like some bread and _____.

2 Is there _____ chicken?

3 There's some meat in the _____.

4 Can I have a _____ sandwich, please?

5 We live on the fourth _____.

6 The river is over _____.

7 Is the window _____ or small?

8 There are _____ posters on my wall.

9 Can I borrow your phone? Sorry, I _____ it.

10 There's a great _____ from my window.

11 Is the street _____ or quiet?

12 We live in a big _____ of flats.

...../11

🎧 5 LISTEN AND CHECK YOUR SCORE	
Total	...../40

26

3 Skills practice

SKILLS FOCUS: READING AND **WRITING**

Read

1 Read the texts quickly and match them to the correct photos.

A ___

Our flat is in a quiet street. It's on the sixth floor, but luckily there's a lift. There are two bedrooms. There's a great view from my bedroom window. The walls in my room are green. There's a clock and a mirror on the walls, but there aren't any posters.

B ___

Our house is a terraced house in the centre of Liverpool. It isn't very quiet, but it's great. There's a living room, a kitchen, a bathroom and there are three bedrooms. The house is 150 years old. There's a garden, but it's very small. There aren't any trees.

C ___

Our flat is on the fourth floor of a block. There isn't a lift! My bedroom is quite big, but the view isn't very good. There's a bed, a wardrobe, a desk and lots of posters on my walls. The flat is very modern and there's a big garden with trees in it for the people here.

2 Read the text again. Match the sentences (1–9) to the texts (A–C).

1 It's on the fourth floor. _C_
2 It's old. ___
3 There are three bedrooms. ___
4 There's a big garden. ___
5 There's a lift. ___

6 There's a great view. ___
7 It's in a quiet road. ___
8 There are posters on his/her walls. ___
9 It's in the centre of the town. ___

Write

3 Rewrite the letter with the correct punctuation.

How are things?

_____

_____

_____

_____

_____

_____

_____

Hi Celina,

how are things our new flat is great There are three bedrooms two bathrooms a kitchen and a living room. Its on the fourth floor. the view is fantastic My room is cool There are lots of posters on the walls lots of books on the shelf and a big desk with a computer on it. how about your room what colour are the walls is there a nice view

Lots of questions Sorry

Love

Melanie

4a Have you got a big family?

Grammar: Regular and irregular noun plurals

1 ⭐ **Complete the sentences with the correct form of the nouns.**

1 I haven't got any _cousins_ (cousin).
2 There are five _____ (child) in my family.
3 I've got three _____ (sister), but I haven't got any _____ (brother).
4 How many _____ (man) are there in your family?
5 My sister and I have got three _____ (uncle) and four _____ (aunt).
6 My _____ (grandparent) are in Canada.
7 The _____ (woman) are in the garden.
8 There are three _____ (person) here.

Vocabulary: Family

2 ⭐ **Read and complete the sentences.**

My dad's parents are Rachel and David.
1 David is my _grandfather_.
2 Rachel is my _____.

My mum's brother is Nigel. His wife is Brenda. They've got one child, Jake.
3 Nigel is my _____.
4 Brenda is my _____.
5 Jake is my _____.

I've got one sister. Her name is Fiona. She's twenty-six and she's got two children, Harry and Susanna.
6 Harry is Fiona's _____.
7 Susanna is Fiona's _____.
8 Harry is my _____.
9 Susanna is my _____.

Terry is my mum's new husband.
10 Terry is my _____.

Grammar: *Have got: I, you, we, they*

3 ⭐ **Complete the sentences and questions with the correct form of *have got*.**

1 I _'ve got_ two brothers. ✓
2 I _____ any sisters. ✗
3 _____ (you) any brothers or sisters?
4 We _____ a dog. ✗
5 _____ (Jake and Sue) any cousins?
6 You _____ a big family. ✓
7 _____ (we) any cousins in America?
8 My uncle and aunt _____ any children. ✗

4 ⭐⭐ **Look at the information about Nathan's family and complete the dialogue.**

Nathan's family:

one brother	no nieces
no sisters	four aunts
two cousins	two uncles
no nephews	

Amber: Hi, Nathan. Can I ask you about your family?
Nathan: Sure.
Amber: [1]_Have you got any_ brothers or sisters?
Nathan: [2]_____ brother, but [3]_____ any sisters.
Amber: [4]_____ any cousins?
Nathan: Yes, [5]_____. [6]_____ cousins.
Amber: [7]_____ any nephews or nieces?
Nathan: No, [8]_____. My brother is only seven years old!
Amber: How many aunts and uncles [9]_____?
Nathan: [10]_____ aunts and two uncles.

Use your English: Talk about your family

5 ⭐ **Choose the correct answer.**

1 A: Have you got any brothers?

B: **Yes, I have.** / Three.

2 A: How many cousins have you got?

B: **Five. / No, I haven't.**

3 A: How old are they?

B: **One's eighteen and one's fifteen. /
They're OK.**

4 A: I've got one brother. How about you?

B: **I'm fine, thanks. / I've got two brothers
and a sister.**

6 ⭐⭐ **Complete the dialogue with one word in
each space.**

Jill: Hi, what's your name?

Kelly: I'm Kelly.

Jill: Hi, Kelly. I'm Jill. This is my party.

Kelly: Oh, right. I'm here with Jake. He's my
cousin.

Jill: Good to meet you. [1] *Have* you got a big
[2]_____?

Kelly: I've got a lot of cousins.

Jill: How [3]_____ cousins have you
[4]_____?

Kelly: About ten.

Jill: Wow. Have you got [5]_____ brothers
or sisters?

Kelly: No, I haven't. I'm an only [6]_____.
How [7]_____ you?

Jill: I've got three brothers, but I haven't got
[8]_____ sisters.

Kelly: How [9]_____ are your brothers?

Jill: One's, twenty-two, one's seventeen and
one's eleven.

Grammar summary

Irregular plurals	
Singular	**Plural**
man	men
woman	women
person	people
child	children

Note

Irregular plurals

- Some plurals are irregular.
  man – men
  woman – women

Common mistakes

~~*I've got two childs.*~~ ✗

I've got two children. ✓

~~*There are three persons here.*~~ ✗

There are three people here. ✓

Have got: I, you, we, they	
Affirmative	**Negative**
I**'ve got** two brothers.	I **haven't got** a sister.
You**'ve got** a big family.	You **haven't got** any posters.
We**'ve got** a cat.	We **haven't got** a dog.
They**'ve got** a big house.	They **haven't got** a red car.
Questions	**Short answers**
Have you **got** a niece?	Yes, I **have.**/No, I **haven't.**
Have I **got** your pen?	Yes, you **have.**/No, you **haven't.**
Have we **got** a menu?	Yes, we **have.**/No, we **haven't.**
Have they **got** any cousins?	Yes, they **have.**/No, they **haven't.**

Note

Use

- We use *have got* to talk about possession.
  They**'ve got** a daughter.
  I**'ve got** a new bike.

Common mistakes

~~**Have you got** a computer? Yes, I've got.~~ ✗

Have you **got** a computer. Yes, I have. ✓

~~You have got a brother?~~ ✗

Have you **got** a brother? ✓

4b She's got brown eyes.

Phrases

1 ⭐ **Complete the dialogue with the phrases from the box.**

> • ~~What's on?~~ • You're just jealous. • Like me!
> • What's she like? • That's for babies.

Angela: Hi, Tom. ¹*What's on?*

Tom: Nancy Drew.

Angela: Nancy Drew! Oh no! ² _____. My little sister has got the DVD.

Tom: It's good. Emma Roberts is in it. She's Julia Roberts' niece.

Angela: Really? ³ _____

Tom: She's nice. She's got long, straight hair and a nice smile.

Angela: ⁴ _____!

Tom: Well, yes …

Angela: But my aunt isn't a film star. That's why she's there and I'm here.

Tom: ⁵ _____, Angela.

Angela: No, I'm not. She's a film star, but I'm here with you!

Vocabulary: Appearance

2 ⭐⭐ **Complete the descriptions with one word in each space.**

She's ¹*young*. She's medium-²h_____.
She's got ³b_____,
⁴c_____ hair and
blue ⁵e_____.

He's ⁶ m_____
-aged. He's good-
⁷l_____. He's got
⁸g_____ hair. He
has got a ⁹ b_____
and a ¹⁰m_____.

Grammar: *Have got: he, she, it*

3 ⭐ **Look at the description of Brian. Then complete the description of Stella.**

Brian's got short, dark hair. He's got brown eyes. He's got a moustache, but he hasn't got a beard.

Stella ¹*'s got* long, fair hair. She ² _____
straight hair. She ³ _____ wavy hair. She
⁴ _____ glasses and she ⁵ _____ a
nice smile.

4 ⭐⭐ **Write the questions.**

Amy: Who's your favourite actress?

Melanie: Well … ask me some questions.

Amy: OK. ¹*Has she got long hair* (long hair)?

Melanie: No … not now.

Amy: ² _____ (What colour hair)?

Melanie: She's got blonde hair. Or red-blonde hair.

Amy: ³ _____ (nice smile)?

Melanie: Yes, she has. Very nice.

Amy: ⁴ _____ (glasses)?

Melanie: No, she hasn't.

Amy: ⁵ _____ (What colour eyes)?

Melanie: She's got brown eyes.

Amy: Is it Emma Watson?

Melanie: Yes, it is.

5 ★★★ Use the prompts to complete the dialogue.

Beth: My favourite actor is Zac Efron.

Danielle: Who?

Beth: He's an actor.

Danielle: [1]*Has he got fair hair or dark hair?* (fair hair or dark hair)?

Beth: Well, in this picture

[2]_____ (fair hair)

Danielle: [3]_____ (nice smile/in this picture)

Beth: [4]_____ (Yes/have)

Danielle: [5]_____ (you/another photo)?

Beth: Yes, I have.

Danielle: Oh, wow! [6]_____ (He/beard and moustache/in this photo)

Beth: Yes.

Danielle: And [7]_____ (he/not/blond hair. He/dark hair).

Beth: That's right.

Danielle: … and [8]_____ (he/not/a nice smile) in this one.

Beth: [9]_____ (No/not). But he's still good-looking.

Grammar summary

Have got: he, she, it

Affirmative	Negative
He's **got** long hair.	He **hasn't got** curly hair.
She's **got** a nice smile.	She **hasn't got** blonde hair.
It's **got** brown eyes.	It **hasn't got** blue eyes.
Questions	**Short answers**
Has he **got** a beard?	Yes, he **has**./No, he **hasn't**.
Has she **got** wavy hair?	Yes, she **has**./No, she **hasn't**.
Has it **got** a big window?	Yes, it **has**./No, it **hasn't**.

Note

Use

- We use *have got* to talk about possession and also to describe someone.
  She's **got** a daughter.
  He's **got** brown hair.

Common mistakes

~~Have she got a big family?~~ ✗

Has she **got** a big family? ✓

4c When's your birthday?

Vocabulary: Months and seasons

1 ⭐ **Put the months in the correct order.**

• May • April • September • ~~January~~
• August • December • October • June
• February • July • November • March

1 *January*   7 _____
2 _____   8 _____
3 _____   9 _____
4 _____   10 _____
5 _____   11 _____
6 _____   12 _____

2 ⭐ **Complete the seasons.**

1 _ _ _ m _ _   2 _ _ r _ _ _

3 _ _ _ t _ _   4 _ _ t _ _ _

3 ⭐⭐ **Write the months that the people's birthdays are in.**

1 Henryk's birthday is in the ninth month.

September

2 Dana's birthday is in the eleventh month.

_____

3 Nadia's birthday is in the second month.

_____

4 Hussein's birthday is in the twelfth month.

_____

5 Claudia's birthday is in the eighth month.

_____

6 Sami's birthday is in the third month.

_____

7 Paula's birthday is in the tenth month.

_____

8 Kostas' birthday is in the fifth month.

_____

Vocabulary: Ordinal numbers

4 ⭐ **Read the text and label the people with their names.**

1 *Max*
2 _____
3 _____
4 _____
5 _____
6 _____
7 _____

My name is Max. This is my block of flats. I live on the seventh floor. My friend Tom is on the third floor. The man on the first floor is Mr Jenkins. He's got my football! My dad's friend, Harry, is on the fifth floor and my mum's cousin, Jack, is on the second floor. The boy on the fourth floor is from Poland. His name's Kuba. The family on the sixth floor are from Canada. That's Jacques in the picture.

5 ⭐⭐ **Change the numbers to words.**

1 The flat is on the *fourth* (4th) floor.
2 My birthday is on the _____ (15th).
3 My mum's birthday is on March _____ (30th).
4 The view from the _____ (21st) floor is fantastic.
5 My dad's birthday is on the _____ (12th).
6 That's your _____ (8th) burger this week!
7 This is my brother's _____ (1st) school trip.
8 We've got a Maths test on the _____ (13th).

Grammar: Prepositions of time: *in, on*

6 ⭐ **Choose the correct words.**

1 My birthday is **in** / **on** May.

2 My birthday is **in** / **on** May 16th.

3 My birthday is **in** / **on** the spring.

4 This year, my birthday is **in** / **on** a Tuesday.

5 Stella's birthday is **in** / **on** December 10th.

6 Stella's birthday is **in** / **on** a Saturday.

7 Stella's birthday is **in** / **on** the winter.

8 Stella's birthday is **in** / **on** December.

7 ⭐⭐ **Answer the questions below.**

Grammar summary

Prepositions of time: *in, on*

My birthday is **in** April/September/May.
The exam is **on** Monday/Wednesday/
 Friday.
The school trip is **in** the summer/winter/
 spring/autumn.
The first day of school is **on** the third of
 September.

Note

- We use **in** with months and seasons.
  The school show is **in** *May. The exams are* **in** *the summer.*

- We use **on** with days of the week and dates.
  My birthday is **on** *Saturday. My birthday is* **on** *the 24th of June.*

1 When's the school show?   *It's in May.*

2 When's your mum's birthday?   _____

3 When's the Maths test?   _____

4 When's the concert?   _____

5 When are the school holidays? _____

4 Language round-up

1 Make the sentences correct by replacing the underlined word.

1 My aunt is my mother's brother. *uncle*

2 There are ten person here. _____

3 That's your three packet of crisps today!

_____

4 My niece is my sister's son. _____

5 What's your sister do? She's tall with long, dark hair. _____

6 Our teacher has got curly eyes. _____

7 My birthday is on the twenty of November.

_____

8 How age is your brother? _____

9 Hi. What's in television today? _____

.../8

2 Complete the dialogue with the words from the box.

> • ¹'ve • child • got • third • eyes • in • Has
> • smile • looking • hasn't • sisters • on

Melissa: Hi, Nathan. How are things?

Nathan: Great. I ¹ *'ve* _____ got a new girlfriend.

Melissa: Fantastic. What's her name?

Nathan: Sara. She's ² _____ long, blonde hair and big, blue ³ _____. She's very good-⁴ _____

Melissa: ⁵ _____ she got glasses?

Nathan: No, she ⁶ _____, but she's got a very nice ⁷ _____.

Melissa: Has she got any brothers or ⁸ _____ ?

Nathan: No. She's an only ⁹ _____.

Melissa: How old is she?

Nathan: She's fifteen. It's her birthday ¹⁰ _____ Monday.

Melissa: Monday. That's the ¹¹ _____ of May. My mum's birthday is ¹² _____ May.

.../11

3 Complete the letter with one word in each space.

Dear Pia,

I've ¹got a big family. There are five ²m_____ – my father, my two grandfathers and two ³u_____. There are seven ⁴w_____ – my mum, two grandmothers and five ⁵a_____. I've got a lot of ⁶c_____, there are fourteen! My mother's sister and her ⁷h_____ have got three sons and two ⁸d_____!

I've got one ⁹b_____. His name's Gary and he's eighteen. He's got short ¹⁰d_____ hair, a ¹¹b_____ and a moustache!

¹²H_____ you got any brothers or sisters? How ¹³m_____ cousins have you got?

Write soon,

Martha

.../12

4 Choose the correct options.

1 **Are you / Have you** got a good place to live?

2 **I've / I've got** a room in south London.

3 Anna's got wavy, blonde **hair / long** and a nice smile.

4 Marianna's got beautiful, big brown **beard / eyes**.

5 She's quite tall with medium- **height / length** dark hair.

6 **How many / How much** students are there?

7 The teacher's name is Annabella. She's **medium / middle** -aged and a very good teacher.

8 We've got an English test **in / on** Thursday.

9 It's our **one / first** test.

10 On August the **fifth / twelve** there's a school trip to Stonehenge.

.../9

🔊 6 LISTEN AND CHECK YOUR SCORE	
Total	.../40

4 Skills practice

SKILLS FOCUS: **READING, LISTENING** AND **WRITING**

Read

1 Read the text quickly and find Elaine in the picture.

15/9 Hi, my name's Elaine and this is my family. I've got one brother. His name is Josh. He's eleven. He's quite annoying and silly. His bedroom is very untidy. His clothes are on the floor and there are books and DVDs on his bed. I haven't got a sister, but I've got a cousin, Donna. She's fourteen, like me, and she's an only child. Luckily, her house is in the street behind our street. We are in the same class at school. She's my best friend.

My dad's name's Ken and his fiftieth birthday is in November. My mum's name is Sylvia. Mum and I have got blonde hair and blue eyes. Dad and Josh have got dark hair and green eyes.

In this photo, we're in Donna's garden with my uncle and aunt, Donna's parents. Donna's mum is cool. Her name's Jemima and she's my mum's sister. She's forty-two and my mum is forty-five.

2 Read the text again and answer the questions.

1 How old is Josh?

He's eleven.

2 Where are Josh's clothes?

_____

3 Has Donna got any brothers or sisters?

_____

4 What colour hair has Elaine's mum got?

_____

5 What colour eyes have Elaine's Dad and brother got?

_____

6 Where are the family in the photo?

_____

Listen

3 🎧 **7** Listen to five conversations. Who is speaking?

1 ⓐ mother and daughter   b) Two friends

2 a) Two brothers   b) father and son

3 a) brother and sister   b) a mother and son

4 a) Two friends   b) Two sisters

5 a) mother, daughter and son

　 b) Two sisters and a brother

4 🎧 **7** Listen again and match the problems to the conversations.

Conversation 1　　　　Dirty clothes

Conversation 2　　　　An annoying brother

Conversation 3　　　　An untidy room

Conversation 4　　　　A school test

Conversation 5　　　　A boy in his sister's room

Write

5 Choose one of the ideas. Complete the sentences.

1 brother/sister/parents

My brother's bedroom is really untidy.

2 money/clothes/laptop

I haven't got _____.

3 today/January/Saturday

Mary's birthday is _____.

4 clothes/books/phone

My sister _____ all the time

5 cousins/brothers or sisters/big family

I haven't got _____.

6 DVD player/smart phone/boyfriend

My sister has got a new _____. I'm jealous!

5a I work in a film studio.

Vocabulary: Jobs

1 ⭐ Complete the jobs.

 marref

1 t*eacher* 2 f_____

sitrat

posh nastitass

3 a_____ 4 s_____
a_____

bluermp

runes

5 p_____ 6 n_____

diblure

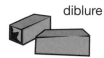

croodt

7 b_____ 8 d_____

Phrases

2 ⭐ Complete the phrases with one word from the box in each space.

• at • OK • right • Cool • look

1 A: I work in a school.
 B: So, you're a teacher?
 A: That's r*ight*_____.

2 A: How much are these earrings?
 B: Don't _____ _____ me! I'm
 not a shop assistant.

3 A: My sister's an artist in Paris.
 B: _____!

4 A: Can you help me?
 B: Yes, _____. What's the problem?

Grammar: Present simple: *I, you, we, they*

3 ⭐ Complete the text with the verbs from the box.

• live • work • come • don't come
• play • speak • don't speak

My name's Antonio. I'm fifteen and I'm at school in London. I ¹ *play* football for the school team.

I ² _____ in London with my parents, but they ³ _____ from London. They ⁴ _____ from Ancona in the east of Italy. They ⁵ _____ as doctors here in London. We live in England, but we ⁶ _____ English at home. We ⁷ _____ Italian because my parents want me to know the language.

4 ⭐⭐ Make the sentences negative.

1 We live in a flat.
 We don't live in a flat.

2 We speak French at home.
 _____

3 I play football for the school team.
 _____

4 Those students come from Chile.
 _____

5 You work as waiters.
 _____

6 My parents come from Greece.
 _____

5 ★★ Complete the short answers.

1 Do you live in Manchester? ✗

  No, I don't.

2 Do your parents come from Spain? ✓

  _____

3 Do you and your friends work on Saturdays? ✗

  _____

4 Do I come from Ireland? ✗

  _____

5 Do you work as a teacher? ✓

  _____

6 Do I live here? ✓

  _____

7 Do your friends play in a band? ✗

  _____

8 Do you and your sister speak Japanese? ✓

  _____

6 ★★★ Use the prompts to complete the dialogue.

Reporter: ¹*Do you work as a musician?*

  (work as/musician?)

Fernando: ² _____ ✓

Reporter: ³ _____

  (where/live?)

Fernando: ⁴ _____

  (Los Angeles)

Reporter: ⁵ _____

  (come from/Los Angeles?)

Fernando: ⁶ _____ ✗

Reporter: ⁷ _____

  (where/come from?)

Fernando: ⁸ _____ (Madrid)

Reporter: ⁹ _____

  (How many languages/speak?)

Fernando: ¹⁰ _____

  (two languages – Spanish and English)

Reporter: ¹¹ _____

  (play/in a band?)

Fernando: ¹² _____ ✓

Grammar summary

Present simple: *I, you, we, they*

Affirmative	Negative
I **work** as a plumber.	I **don't work** as a plumber.
You **speak** Chinese.	You **don't speak** Chinese.
We **come** from Australia.	We **don't come** from Australia.
They **play** tennis.	They **don't play** tennis.

Questions	Short answers
Do you **speak** Russian?	Yes, I **do**./No, I **don't**.
Do I **work** for you?	Yes, you **do**./No, you **don't**.
Do we **live** here?	Yes, we **do**./No, we **don't**.
Do they **come** from Poland?	Yes, they **do**./No, they **don't**.

Note

Use

- We use the present simple to talk about things which are facts or always true.
  I come from Nottingham.

Form

- In affirmative sentences, *I*, *you*, *we* and *they* all take the same form.
  I/We/You/They speak French.
- We use *don't* to make negatives.
  *I/We/You/They **don't speak** French.*
- In questions the word order is *Do* + subject + main verb + ?
  ***Do** you **play** tennis?*
- We use *do/don't* in short answers. We do not repeat the main verb.
  ***Do** you **live** here? Yes, I **do**./No, I **don't**.*
  NOT ~~Yes, I do live. Yes, I live. No, I don't live.~~

Common mistakes

~~I not speak Italian~~ ✗
I **don't speak** Italian. ✓
~~Where you work?~~ ✗
Where **do** you **work**? ✓

5b He works on the beach.

Grammar: Present simple: *he, she, it*

1 ★ **Complete the sentences with the correct form of the verbs.**

1 My dad *works* (work) in a hospital.

2 Ben _____ (play) football on Saturdays.

3 My sister _____ (want) to go to America.

4 My mum _____ (come) from Brazil.

5 Simon _____ (not work) here.

6 Casey _____ (not speak) Portuguese.

7 Patrice _____ (not come) from France.

2 ★★ **Complete the dialogue with the correct form of the verbs from the box.**

> • come (x2) • live • not live • ~~play~~ (x3)
> • speak (x2)

A: My favourite sports star is Oscar.

B: What sport ¹*does* he *play*?

A: He ² _____ football.

B: Where ³ _____ he _____ from?

A: He ⁴ _____ from Brazil, but he ⁵ _____
in Brazil now. He ⁶ _____ in London because he
⁷ _____ football for Chelsea.

B: What languages ⁸ _____ he _____?

A: He ⁹ _____ Portuguese and a little English.

3 ★★ **Look at the information and complete the sentences.**

	Akari	Joaquin
From	Tokyo, Japan	Santiago, Chile
Now in	Paris, France	Madrid, Spain
Languages	Japanese, French, English	Spanish, Portuguese, Italian
Job	Artist	Electrician

Akari ¹*comes* from Tokyo in Japan, but she ² _____
in Japan. She ³ _____ in Paris now. She ⁴ _____
three languages, Japanese, French and English. Akari
⁵ _____ as an artist. She's a very good artist.

Joaquin ⁶ _____ from Tokyo. He ⁷ _____ from
Santiago, in Chile. He ⁸ _____ in Chile now. He
⁹ _____ in Madrid, in Spain. He ¹⁰ _____ English,
but he ¹¹ _____ Spanish, Portuguese and Italian.

Joaquin ¹² _____ as an electrician.

4 ★★★ **Rewrite the dialogue using *she*.**

A: What's your name?

B: My name's Amy.

A: Where do you live?

B: I live in Perth.

A: Do you come from Perth?

B: No, I don't. I come from Glasgow.

A: What do you do?

B: I work as a teacher.

A: Do you play a sport?

B: Yes, I do. I play tennis.

A: What languages do you speak?

B: I speak English and a little French.

A: This is Amy.

B: ¹*Where does she live?*

A: She ² _____

B: ³ _____

A: ⁴ _____

B: ⁵ _____

A: ⁶ _____

B: ⁷ _____

A: ⁸ _____

B: ⁹ _____

A: ¹⁰ _____

Vocabulary: Places of work

5 ⭐ **Match the people to the places they work. Some places match with more than one person.**

1 factory worker	a) school
2 nurse	b) shop
3 builder	c) office
4 farmer	d) restaurant
5 secretary	e) factory
6 waitress	f) farm
7 doctor	g) building site
8 teacher	h) hospital
9 shop assistant	
10 chef	

6 ⭐⭐ **Complete the sentences with the places the people work.**

1 I'm a teacher in a big s_chool_ in Portsmouth.

2 I work as a housewife so I work in my h_____.

3 My mum is a nurse, but she doesn't work in a h_____. She's a school nurse.

4 I work as a waiter in a Chinese r_____.

5 They are workers in a f_____. They make toys there.

6 My uncle's a builder. He works on a b_____ s_____.

7 My mum works in an o_____. She isn't a secretary, but she has got a secretary.

8 My dad is a farmer. He's got animals on his f_____.

Grammar summary

Present simple: *he, she, it*	
Affirmative	**Negative**
He **takes** photographs. She **works** in an office. It **takes** three hours.	He **doesn't take** photographs. She **doesn't work** in an office. It **doesn't take** three hours.
Questions	**Short answers**
Does he live in England? **Does** she come from China? **Does** it take a long time?	Yes, he **does**./No, he **doesn't**. Yes, she **does**./No, she **doesn't**. Yes, it **does**./No, it **doesn't**.

Note

Use

- We use the present simple to talk about things which are facts or always true.
  He speaks Polish.

Form

- In affirmative sentences, *he*, *she* and *it* all take the same form.
  *He/She/It **comes** from Italy.*
- We use *doesn't* to make negatives.
  *He/She/It **doesn't live** here.*
- In questions the word order is *Does* + subject + main verb + ?
  ***Does** she **work** outside?*
- In questions and negatives, we do not add an -*s* to the main verb, only to the verb *do*.
  ***Does** he **work** here?* NOT ~~*Does he works here?*~~
  *She **doesn't speak** Spanish.* NOT ~~*She doesn't speaks Spanish.*~~
- We use *does/doesn't* in short answers. We do not repeat the main verb.
  ***Does** he **live** here? Yes, he **does**./No, he **doesn't**.*
  NOT ~~*Yes, he does live. Yes, he lives. No, he doesn't live.*~~

Common mistakes

~~*She speak Italian*~~ ✗
*She **speaks** Italian.* ✓
~~*What she does?*~~ ✗
*What **does** she **do**?* ✓

Spelling rules

- We add -*es* to make third person singular affirmative forms after verbs ending in:
  -o – do → *does*
  -ch – watch → *watches*
  -ss – pass → *passes*
- When a verb ends in a consonant + -*y*, we change the -*y* to -*i* and add -*es*. When a verb ends in a vowel + -*y*, we add -*s*.
  study → *studies*
  play → *plays*

5c Do you like her?

Grammar: Object pronouns: *me, you, him, her, it, us, them*

1 ⭐ **Match the responses to the questions.**

What do you think of ...

1 Sandra Bullock? <u>d</u>
2 me? __
3 the students in class 4C? __
4 homework? __
5 Mr Smith, our Maths teacher? __

What does your girlfriend think of ...

6 you? __
7 your parents? __
8 you and your friends? __
9 ice cream? __
10 your sister? __

a) I hate it.
b) She loves it.
c) I like him.
d) I like her.
e) She likes us.
f) I love you!
g) She likes them.
h) I don't like them.
i) She doesn't like her.
j) She loves me.

2 ⭐⭐ **Make sentences.**

 = love   ◉◉ = like

◉◉ = not keen on   ✗ = hate

1 bananas 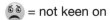 *I'm not keen on them.*

2 summer

_____

3 onions ✗

_____

4 fast food

_____

5 my grandmother

_____

6 my cousin's boyfriend ◉◉

_____

Vocabulary: Adjectives of opinion

3 ⭐ **Choose the correct words.**

1 I don't like beards. They're **awful** / **great**.
2 I hate winter. It's **fantastic** / **terrible**.
3 I love my mobile phone. It's **weird** / **fantastic**.
4 I really like your earrings. They're **cool** / **boring**.
5 My friend loves sport. He thinks it's **brilliant** / **bad**.
6 My parents think rap music is **awful** / **good**. They hate it.
7 My boyfriend likes football, but I think it's **great** / **boring**.
8 I don't like these sandwiches. They aren't very **good** / **bad**.
9 This film is **funny** / **weird**. I don't like it.

4 ⭐⭐ **Complete the words.**

Adam: I hate it here. These sculptures are ¹a<u>wful</u>.
Beth: No, they aren't. They're
²f __ __ __ __ s __ __ __. Look at this. It's
³b __ __ l __ __ __ n __.
Adam: Why? What's ⁴g __ __ __ __ about it? It isn't
interesting at all. It's ⁵b __ __ __ n __. I want to go
to the cinema.
Beth: The cinema?
Adam: Yes. There's a good film on. It's very ⁶f __ __ __ y.

Beth:	Do you mean *Hi, Mum, I'm Home*?
Adam:	Yes. Adam Chandler is in it. He's really [7]c __ __ l.
Beth:	That's a [8]t __ __ __ __ b __ __ film. Really [9]b __ __. And he isn't a [10]g __ __ d actor!

Use your English: Exchange opinions

5 ★ **Complete the dialogue with one word in each space.**

Stella:	What do you [1]*think* of the Harry Potter films?
Mark:	I like [2]_____. I think [3]_____ are great.
Stella:	Me [4]_____. What [5]_____ you, Debbie? [6]_____ you like them?
Debbie:	Not really, but I love the books.

6 ★★ **Find two dialogues and put them in the correct order.**

Really? I love it. What about you, James? Do you like it?

What do you think of *Twilight*, Ellen?

Not really. I think she's boring.

~~What do you think of Adele, Sam?~~

Yes, I think it's cool.

I think she's great.

I don't like it. I think it's weird.

Me too. I love her music.

What about you, Kate? Do you like her?

Dialogue 1

A: [1]*What do you think of Adele, Sam?*

B: [2]_____

A: [3]_____

B: [4]_____

C: [5]_____

Dialogue 2

D: [6]_____

E: [7]_____

D: [8]_____

F: [9]_____

Grammar summary

Object pronouns

Subject pronouns	Object pronouns
I	**me**
you	**you**
he	**him**
she	**her**
it	**it**
we	**us**
they	**them**

Note

- We use object pronouns after verbs and prepositions.
  *Jane likes crisps. Jane likes **them**.*
  *That's my cake. It's for **me**.*
- We use *you* for singular and plurals.
  *I love **you**, Helen.*
  *Mark, Steve. Mum wants **you**.*

5 Language round-up

1 Find the mistakes. Rewrite the sentences correctly.

1 Where you live?

Where do you live?

2 What your father does?

_____

3 Jake not like English.

_____

4 Our parents love we very much.

_____

5 Cathy work as a teacher.

_____

6 I not like French.

_____

7 Where are my books? I can't see it.

_____

8 This is my grandfather. I love her very much.

_____

9 Does Jim likes rap music?

_____

…/8

2 Use the prompts to write answers to the questions.

1 A: Do you like this song?

B: *No, I don't. I hate it. It's terrible.* (don't/hate/terrible)

2 A: What do you think of Gary?

B: _____. (like him/cool)

3 A: Do you like One Direction?

B: _____! (do not/awful)

4 A: What does your mum think of your new girlfriend?

B: _____. (like)

5 A: Where does Anna come from?

B: _____, but

_____. (Russia/not live/Russia now)

6 A: Does your dad like his job?

B: _____. (no/hate)

7 A: What do you think of music festivals?

B: _____. (I/not/keen/on)

…/12

3 Look at the information in the chart and the dialogue. Write similar dialogues for the other people.

	Magda	Tomas	Maria and Penelope
live now	London	Paris	Lisbon
come from	Poland	Russia	Argentina
work	hospital	in an office	in a school

Magda

A: Where does Magda live?

B: She lives in London.

A: Where does she come from?

B: She comes from Poland.

A: Does she work in an office?

B: No, she doesn't. She works in a hospital.

Tomas

A: ¹*Where does Tomas live?*

B: ²*He lives in Paris.*

A: ³_____

B: ⁴_____

A: ⁵_____ in an office?

B: ⁶_____

Maria and Penelope

A: ¹_____

B: ²_____

A: ³_____

B: ⁴_____

A: ⁵_____ in an office?

B: ⁶_____.

_____ school.

…/20

LISTEN AND CHECK YOUR SCORE	
Total	…/40

5 Skills practice

SKILLS FOCUS: READING WRITING

Read

1 Read the text quickly. Match the adjectives to the nouns.

1 Christmas	a) television
2 big	b) children
3 nice	c) tips
4 noisy	d) flat
5 expensive	e) food

My name's Frank and I'm fourteen years old. I'm a paperboy. I work from 7 a.m. until 8 a.m. from Monday to Friday. Then I go to school. I don't like my job, but I like the money. At Christmas, I get a lot of tips.

My friend Max works as a cleaner in a restaurant. He works on Saturdays from 11 a.m. until 6 p.m. He gets £4 an hour, but he doesn't get tips. He likes his work.

My sister, Rachel, works as a babysitter. She does it on Fridays and Saturdays. The people she works for have got a big television and there is a lot of nice food like biscuits and crisps. She gets £10 for an evening. The only bad thing is that the children are noisy.

My cousin, Teresa, works as a shop assistant. She's 19 and she's at university. She works in the evenings and she gets £120 a week! She doesn't like her work, but she lives in a flat and it's expensive.

2 Read the text again and answer the questions.

Who

1 cleans a place? *Max*

2 doesn't like his/her job?_____,
_____

3 works in the evenings? _____,
_____

4 only works in the morning? _____

5 works one day a week? _____

6 works with children? _____

Write

3 Choose the correct words.

1 I like babysitting [because] / so / but I like children.

2 I like the people I work with but / and / because the customers.

3 It's a busy restaurant but / because / so we work very hard.

4 I haven't got a job this year because / so / but we've got a lot of exams at school.

5 The pay isn't very good, and / because / but we get a lot of tips.

6 It's a big office so / but / because it takes a long time to clean.

4 Complete the email with the phrases from the box.

- I get £5 an hour • I don't like it
- she wants to learn the language
- I want to work outside in the summer
- she doesn't speak much English
- we get food • we're always busy
- the bedrooms are always really messy

Hi Hannah,
How are things? I've got a new job, but
¹*I don't like it*. I'm a cleaner in a big hotel. It's annoying because ²_____. Like my brother's bedroom! The girl I work with is nice, but ³_____. She's in England because ⁴_____.
There's a lot to do so ⁵_____. We work inside. It's nice in the winter, but ⁶_____.
I work from 7 a.m. until 3 p.m. on Saturdays and Sundays and ⁷_____. That's £80 a week!! We don't get tips, but ⁸_____.
I hope you like your job in the pizza restaurant.
Love
Gina

6a When does it leave?

Phrases

1 ⭐ **Complete the dialogues with one word in each space.**

1 **A:** Good morning.

B: It's ten o'clock. The tour starts in an hour.

A: Oh. What d<u>o</u> you t _____? Have I got time for breakfast?

B: Yes, I think s_____, but h_____ u_____.

2 **A:** This isn't a typical hotel.

B: What d_____ you m_____?

A: There are ghosts here.

Vocabulary: Clock times

2 ⭐ **Choose the correct times.**

1 (a) It's twenty past nine.

b) It's quarter past nine.

2 a) It's quarter to eight.

b) It's quarter past seven.

3 a) It's ten to five.

b) It's five to five.

4 a) It's three past ten.

b) It's ten past three.

5 a) It's half past six.

b) It's half to seven.

6 a) It's twelve minutes past twelve.

b) It's twelve o'clock.

7 a) It's twenty-five past two.

b) It's twenty-five to three.

8 a) It's quarter past eight.

b) It's quarter to eight.

3 ⭐⭐ **Write the times in sentences.**

1 6.00   _It's six o'clock._

2 9.55   _____

3 21.45   _____

4 00.40   _____

5 8.30   _____

6 14.10   _____

7 18.35   _____

8 3.15   _____

Grammar: Present simple with fixed times

4 ⭐ **Choose the correct options.**

1 The bus [leaves] / opens / finishes at 6.30.

2 Paul's train **closes** / **starts** / **arrives** at 11.30.

3 The museum **starts** / **opens** / **finishes** at 10.00.

4 What time does the tour **finish** / **close** / **arrive**?

5 Does the match **open** / **start** / **arrive** at 3 p.m.?

6 The ticket office **finishes** / **leaves** / **closes** at 17.30.

7 When does the last boat **leave** / **finish** / **close**?

8 The train to London leaves **on** / **in** / **at** four o'clock.

5 ⭐⭐ **Complete the sentences with the correct form of the verbs from the box.**

- open • close • ~~start~~ • finish
- arrive • leave

1 Quick. Our test _starts_ in ten minutes. I don't want to be late.

2 You haven't got time to buy crisps. Our train _____ in two minutes!

3 'Go to bed!' 'Oh, Mum. This film _____ in five minutes. Can I go to bed then?'

4 The shops near the school _____ at eight o'clock in the morning so we buy sandwiches there for lunch.

5 I get the school bus at 8.10 a.m. It _____ at school at 8.35 a.m. so I have lots of time to talk to my friends before my first lesson.

6 ⭐ **Look at the information and complete the questions and answers.**

BUS TOURS: ⟩⟩

9.00–11.30
12.00–14.30
15.00–17.30

BOATS TO GREENWICH

Westminster	Greenwich
11.00	13.15
13.30	14.45
15.00	16.15

MUSEUM

Monday–Friday	9.00–17.30
Saturday	9.00–21.30
Sunday	10.00–16.00

GHOST TOUR
20.30–22.15

A: What time/first bus tour/start?

¹*What time does the first bus tour start?*

B: It ² _____

A: Is there a boat to Greenwich from Westminster?

B: Yes, there is.

A: What time/leave?

³ _____

B: first boat/leave/and the last boat/leave

⁴ _____

A: When/last boat/arrive?

⁵ _____

B: It ⁶ _____.

A: What time/museum/open/Sunday?

⁷ _____

B: It ⁸ _____.

A: What time/close?

⁹ _____

B: It ¹⁰ _____.

A: Oh, great. A ghost tour. When/start?

¹¹ _____

B: start/and finish

¹² It _____.

Grammar summary

Present simple with fixed times

The museum **opens** at nine o'clock.
The shop **closes** at 6 p.m.
The boat **leaves** at 3.30 p.m.
The bus **arrives** at 11.40 a.m.
The tour **starts** at 11.15 a.m.
The match **finishes** at 4.45 p.m.

Note
- We use the present simple to talk about times or things that happen regularly.
  School starts at nine o'clock.
  *The museum **closes** at 6 p.m.*

Common mistakes
~~What time the shops open?~~ ✗
What time **do** the shops **open**. ✓
~~The bus leave at 4 p.m.~~ ✗
The bus **leaves** at 4 p.m. ✓

Preposition of time: *at*

The match starts **at** four o'clock.
The bus leaves **at** 11.40 a.m.

Note
- We use the preposition *at* before clock times.
  *I start work **at** 8 a.m.*

Common mistakes
~~School starts on 9 a.m.~~ ✗
School starts **at** 9 a.m. ✓

6b I usually have fish.

Vocabulary: Daily routines

1 ⭐ Complete the activities with the correct verb.

1 *have* breakfast

2 _____ to bed

3 _____ home

4 _____ in bed

5 _____ your friends

6 _____ your homework

7 _____ your teeth

8 _____ a shower

9 _____ to music

10 _____ lunch

11 _____ school

12 _____ television

Grammar: Adverbs of frequency

2 ⭐ Make sentences.

1 get up | o'clock | I | at | always | eight
   I always get up at eight o'clock.

2 in | I | watch TV | never | the evening
   _____

3 read | I | ever | in bed | hardly
   _____

4 My | rap music | dad | listens to | sometimes
   _____

5 late | is | My brother | for school | often
   _____

6 I | a shower | have | in | usually | the morning
   _____

7 boring | never | English | are | lessons
   _____

8 We | have | Fridays | pizza | on | always
   _____

3 ★★ **Look at the information and write sentences.**

1 Have sandwiches for lunch

Me – always

My friend – never

I always have sandwiches for lunch.

My friend never has sandwiches for lunch.

2 Get up 6.30 a.m.

My parents – always

Me – never

_____

_____

3 Be late for school

Me – hardly ever

My sister – sometimes

_____

_____

4 Surf the net

Me – often

My parents – hardly ever

_____

_____

5 Be messy

My room – always

My sister's room – never

_____

_____

4 ★★★ **Make sentences using the word in brackets.**

1 A: Are you often late for school?

B: Yes, *I'm always late for school*. (always)

C: No, _____ (never).

2 A: Do you often watch TV in the evening?

B: No, _____ (we/never).

A: What do you do?

B: _____

(always/homework and then usually/read).

3 A: What does your brother do in the evening?

B: _____

(usually/computer games).

4 A: Does your dad cook dinner?

B: Yes, _____ (always).

A: Does your mum always help him?

B: No, _____ (hardly ever).

Grammar summary

Adverbs of frequency

I **always** go to bed at ten o'clock.

My sister **usually** has breakfast at home.

We **often** go to school by bus.

My parents **sometimes** go to the theatre.

I **hardly ever** watch television.

We are **never** late for school.

Note

- We use adverbs of frequency to describe how often someone does something or how often something happens.

Form

- Adverbs of frequency come after the verb *to be*.

  He **is often** tired.

  They **are never** happy.

- Adverbs of frequency come before other verbs.

  He **hardly ever goes** to bed at ten o'clock.

  We **sometimes have** burgers for lunch.

- *sometimes* can also come at the start or the end of a sentence.

  Sometimes, I do my homework in the kitchen.

  I do my homework in the kitchen **sometimes.**

Common mistakes

~~He always is late.~~ ✗

He is **always** late. ✓

5 A: Does your teacher go to school by bus?

B: No, he _____ (never).

A: How does he go to school?

B: _____ (usually/car).

47

6c Once a week.

Grammar: Adverbial phrases of frequency

1 ⭐ **Match the phrases (1–7) to the phrases (a–g) which have the same meaning.**

1 once a week	a on the last day of the month
2 twice a day	b in April, August and December
3 three times a year	c on Monday and Thursday
4 twice a month	d in May
5 once a year	e every Saturday
6 once a month	f on the 10th and on the 23rd
7 twice a week	g when I get up and when I go to bed

2 ⭐⭐ **Complete the sentences with one word in each space.**

1 We have homework _every_ day. It's not fair!

2 We have drama club _____ a week, on Mondays.

3 We have exams at school _____ a year, in January and in June.

4 I brush my teeth _____ times a day. When I get up, after breakfast and when I go to bed.

5 My brother plays computer games _____ evening for an hour.

6 We have football practice _____ a week, on Tuesdays and Thursdays.

7 We go to France _____ summer.

8 There is a school show _____ a year, in June.

3 ⭐⭐ **One word in each sentence is wrong. Cross out the wrong word and write the correct one.**

1 I go to the cinema ~~one~~ a week.

once

2 How many do you go shopping?

_____

3 We have homework ever day.

_____

4 I meet my friends two a week.

_____

5 We have a holiday once the year.

_____

6 I go to French classes three time a week.

_____

4 ⭐⭐ **Complete the sentences with the words in the box.**

- a • every (x2) • How • year • ~~often~~
- Once • Twice • week

A: How ^{1}_often_ do you go shopping?

B: I go shopping ^{2}_____ Saturday. What about you?

A: I hardly ever go shopping. I go about once ^{3}_____ month. I hate shopping.

B: Really? I love it.

A: I know!

B: What do you do at the weekend?

A: I go to the cinema ^{4}_____ Friday and, on Saturdays, I usually watch TV or surf the internet. Oh, and I do my homework. ^{5}_____ a ^{6}_____, on Sunday, I visit my grandmother.

B: ^{7}_____ often does she visit you?

A: ^{8}_____ a ^{9}_____. At Christmas and on my mum's birthday. She hasn't got a car.

Use your English: Express surprise and comment

5 ⭐ **Complete the dialogues with one word in each space.**

1 A: I cook dinner every Saturday.

  B: That's g<u>ood</u>.

2 A: I go swimming every day.

  B: E_____ day? You're j_____!

3 A: We never have homework at the weekend.

  B: R_____? That's not fair. We get a lot.

4 A: My brother is late for school every day.

  B: That's n_____ very good.

5 A: I go to Italian classes twice a week.

  B: T_____'s great. Well d_____.

6 A: There's an old film on at our cinema every Thursday.

  B: That's i_____.

6 ⭐ **Number the conversation in the correct order.**

☐ a) **Alfie:** A concert? Wow! Well done.

☐ b) **Alfie:** I eat it every day.

☐ c) **Alfie:** Once a year. I go swimming on holiday.

☐ d) **Alfie:** Really? No TV? That's interesting. What do you do in the evenings?

☐ e) **Alfie:** Wow! That's great. And how often do you watch TV?

☐ f) **Oliver:** Every day? You're joking! That's awful. How often do you take exercise?

☐ 1 g) **Oliver:** How often do you eat fast food?

☐ h) **Oliver:** I play the piano. I'm in a concert next week.

☐ i) **Oliver:** Never. We haven't got a TV.

☐ 11 j) **Oliver:** Thanks. Do you want to come and see me?

☐ k) **Oliver:** That's not very good. I take exercise every day.

Grammar summary

Adverbial phrases of frequency

I have a shower	once a day.
I drink coffee	twice a day.
I brush my teeth	three times a day.
I go to the cinema	once a week.
I go to football practice	twice a month.
We visit my aunt	three times a year.
I phone my friends	every day.
I go shopping	every Saturday.

Note

- Adverbial phrases of frequency always come after the activity they describe.
  *I eat crisps **three times a week**.*
  *She goes to the cinema **every Sunday**.*

Asking about frequency

How often do I/you/we/they cook dinner?
How often does he/she/it eat fast food?
How often am I late?
How often are you/we/they tired?
How often is he/she/it the first to arrive?

Note

- To ask about frequency using the verb *to be*, we use:
  How often + verb to be (is/am/are) + subject + adjective
  ***How often are** you late?*
- To ask about frequency using other verbs, we use:
  How often + do/does + subject + verb
  ***How often do** you **play** tennis?*
  ***How often does** Sam **eat** breakfast?*

6 Language round-up

1 Match the beginnings (1–12) to the endings (a–l).

1 It's twelve	a) ever have tests.
2 I brush my	b) bed.
3 I always do	c) TV in the evening.
4 I have a	d) lunch at school.
5 My sister has	e) past eight.
6 I never listen	f) day.
7 I never watch	g) o'clock.
8 We hardly	h) some emails.
9 I ride my bike every	i) teeth every day.
10 I want to write	j) my homework.
11 It's half	k) to music.
12 My dad reads in	l) shower every day.

…/11

2 Use the prompts. Write questions and answers.

1 A: often/you/late for school?

B: never/late for school

A: How often are you late for school?

B: I'm never late for school.

2 A: When/your/English lesson finish?

B: It/finish/half/three

A: _____

B: _____

3 A: often/your brother/surf the net?

B: He/surf/the net/five/week

A: _____

B: _____

4 A: What time/the museum/close?

B: It/close/six/clock

A: _____

B: _____

5 A: What/you/usually do/weekend?

B: usually/hang out/friends

A: _____

B: _____

6 A: your dad/read in bed?

B: no/never/read/in bed

A: _____

B: _____

…/10

3 Complete the dialogue with words from the box.

• does • always • at • often • ~~usually~~
• to • arrive • Twice • ever • start • half

Meg: Hello, Sam. I don't [1]*usually* see you here.

Sam: No, I hardly [2]_____ go to school by bus. What time [3]_____ it usually [4]_____?

Meg: At [5]_____ past eight.

Sam: But it's twenty-five [6]_____ nine now.

Meg: Don't worry. The bus is [7]_____ late. It's OK. Lessons [8]_____ at nine.

Sam: I know. It's Italian [9]_____ nine o'clock.

Meg: I go to Italian lessons.

Sam: Do you? How [10]_____ do you go?

Meg: [11]_____ a week on Tuesdays and Thursdays.

Sam: Say something in Italian.

Meg: L'autobus è qui.

Sam: What does that mean?

Meg: The bus is here. Look!

…/10

4 Choose the correct options.

My brother is awful. He never [1]does / **makes** / **gets** his homework and he hardly [2]**never** / **every** / **ever** tidies his room. He gets [3]**up** / **out** / **off** late and he never [4]**has** / **does** / **goes** breakfast. He gets [5]**to home** / **home** / **for home** late and he goes to his bedroom. He listens [6]**music** / **the music** / **to music** and he surfs [7]**a net** / **the net** / **net**. He doesn't [8]**make** / **do** / **have** his homework and he has a shower about once [9]**a** / **in** / **for** a week and he goes [10]**bed** / **in bed** / **to bed** very late. He's really annoying!!

…/9

🎧 LISTEN AND CHECK YOUR SCORE

Total	…/40

6 Skills practice

SKILLS FOCUS: READING, LISTENING AND WRITING

Read

1 Read the texts and match them to the photos.

A

Come on a river boat tour today! Boats leave from behind the Park Hotel at 11 a.m., 2 p.m. and 5 p.m. On Saturdays, there is also a boat at 8 p.m. Tickets are £5 from the ticket office. Ask for a leaflet at the ticket office or at the hotel.

B

Our new museum is open every day and tickets for the castle and the museum together are only £3. A ticket for the museum only is £2. There are lots of interesting things to see and there is a café with good food and hot and cold drinks.

C

Every evening*, we walk to the old castle to look for … GHOSTS! We leave at 8.30 p.m. and come back at about one o'clock in the morning. You need food, drinks and a camera. Have a fantastic time with us. The tour is free, but don't be late!

*Not Sundays

2 Read the text again. Answer true (T), false (F) or doesn't say (DS).

1 There are three boat tours every day. _T_

2 The last boat tour on Saturdays is at 5 p.m. ___

3 The new museum is great for children. ___

4 You can see the museum and the castle for £3. ___

5 There is a ghost tour six days a week. ___

6 The people always see ghosts on the tour. ___

Listen

3 Look at the text in Exercise 4. Match the spaces in the text to the types of information.

Day of the week   _1_

Times   __, __, __, __

Prices   __, __, __, __

Preposition of place   __

4 🎧10 Listen to the conversation and complete the information.

CROSBY CASTLE

Opens: Every day (not [1] _Sunday_)
[2] _____

Closes: [3] _____ (Last tour
[4] _____)

Tickets: Castle only: [5] _____
([6] _____ for children)

Castle tour: [7] _____ ([8] _____ for children)

French tour: Every day at [9] _____
Tickets from the ticket office
[10] _____ the castle or online.

Write

5 Complete the text with the words from the box.

> • at • finishes • free • gets • leaves • ~~on~~
> • starts

My brother's got a part-time job in a restaurant. He works [1]_on_ Saturdays and Sundays. He [2]_____ work at nine o'clock in the morning and [3]_____ at four o'clock in the afternoon. My brother goes to work by bus. The bus [4]_____ at half past eight. He [5]_____ to work [6]_____ five to nine. He's never late for work. He likes his job. He gets £6 an hour and he gets [7]_____ pizza!

7a What are you doing?

Phrases

1 ⭐ **Complete the dialogue with the words from the box.**

> • not • weather • bet • ~~lucky~~
> • believe • horrible • like

Annie: Hi, Jo. How's Spain?

Jo: Great.

Annie: We're having a barbecue today.

Jo: ¹*Lucky* you. What's the ²_____ ³_____?

Annie: It's ⁴_____! Rain, rain, rain. I ⁵_____ it's sunny where you are.

Jo: Well, actually, ⁶_____ it or ⁷_____, it's raining here too.

Annie: Really?

Jo: No, not really. It's beautiful!

Grammar: Present continuous

2 ⭐ **Complete the sentences with the correct form of a verb from the box.**

> • ~~write~~ • shop • sleep • eat • talk
> • watch • do • play • cook

1 My sister is at her desk. She *'s writing* an email.

2 My parents are in the kitchen. They _____ dinner.

3 I'm in my bedroom. I _____ my homework.

4 Mrs Jones is in the town centre. She _____.

5 My uncle isn't in bed, but he _____.

6 My friends are happy. They _____ computer games.

7 My dog is in the kitchen. He _____ his dinner.

8 My sister has got a new mobile phone. She _____ to her friend.

9 We are in the living room. We _____ television.

3 ⭐⭐ **Complete the sentences with the correct form of the verbs in brackets.**

1 Girl: Mum! *Tom's playing* (Tom/play) computer games!

   Tom: _____ (I/not/play) computer games. _____ (I/do) my homework!

2 Boy: Mum! _____ (Becky/talk) to James on her phone.

   Becky: _____ (I/not/talk) to James. _____ (I/talk) to Emily.

3 Children: Mum! _____ (Dad/eat) your cakes.

   Dad: _____ (I/not/eat) your cakes. _____ (I/make) dinner.

4 Boy: Mum! _____ (Dan and Ed/use) my computer.

   Boys: _____ (We/not/use) your computer. _____ (We/look) for our computer game.

4 ★★★ Complete the questions and answers.

1 A: you/make/a cake?

B: No/not. I/cook/dinner.

A: *Are you making a cake?*

B: *No, I'm not. I'm cooking dinner.*

2 A: your brother/have/a shower?

B: No/not. He/have/breakfast

A: _____

B: _____

3 A: your parents/watch/TV?

B: No/not. They/listen/to music

A: _____

B: _____

4 A: your sister/do/her homework?

B: No/not. She/surf/the internet

A: _____

B: _____

5 A: you and your friends/go/to school?

B: No/not. We/play/football

A: _____

B: _____

6 A: it/rain?

B: No/not. The sun/shine

A: _____

B: _____

Vocabulary: The weather

5 ★ Complete the sentences with the weather.

1 It's 35°C today. It's really h_ot_.

2 The garden is white! It's s_____.

3 There are a lot of clouds today. It's very c_____.

4 It's 20°C today. It's nice and w_____.

5 Oh no! It's r_____. We can't play tennis today.

6 Look! It's –20°C today. It's f_____!

7 I can't see the house across the street because it's very f_____ today.

8 What a lovely day. There aren't any clouds. It's s_____. The sun is s_____ and I'm going to the beach!

9 Take your hat. It's _____ today, only 5°C.

Grammar summary

Present continuous

Affirmative	Negative
I'm watching TV.	I'm not watching TV.
You're cooking dinner.	You aren't cooking dinner.
He's playing tennis.	He isn't playing tennis.
She's doing her homework.	She isn't doing her homework.
It's raining.	It isn't raining.
We're talking.	We aren't talking.
They're eating burgers.	They aren't eating burgers.

Questions	Short answers
Are you sitting here?	Yes, I am./No, I'm not.
Am I helping you?	Yes, you are./No, you aren't
Is he working?	Yes, he is./No, he isn't.
Is she having lunch?	Yes, she is./No, she isn't.
Is the sun shining?	Yes, it is./No, it isn't.
Are we making a cake?	Yes, we are./No we aren't.
Are they watching us?	Yes, they are./No, they aren't.

Note

Use

- We use the present continuous to talk about things which are happening now.

Common mistakes

She's eat lunch. ✗

She's eating lunch. ✓

He playing computer games. ✗

He's playing computer games. ✓

What you are doing? ✗

What are you doing? ✓

Spelling rules for -ing forms.

- For most verbs, we add -ing.
  go – going
- When a verb ends in -e, we take away the -e.
  make – making
- When a verb ends in -ie, we change the -ie to -y.
  lie – lying
- When a verb ends with one vowel and one consonant, we usually double the final consonant.
  swim – swimming

7b I'm visiting my friends.

Vocabulary: Sports

1 ⭐ **Complete the sports with one letter in each space.**

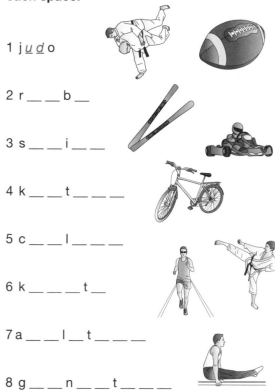

1 j u _d_ o

2 r _ _ b _

3 s _ _ i _ _

4 k _ _ t _ _ _ _

5 c _ _ l _ _ _ _

6 k _ _ _ t _

7 a _ _ l _ t _ _ _ _

8 g _ _ n _ _ t _ _ _

Grammar: Present simple and present continuous

2 ⭐ **Complete the sentences with the correct form of the verbs in brackets.**

At the moment, …

1 I _'m playing_ (play) basketball.

2 we _____ (watch) a football match.

Every week, …

3 my dad _____ (go) swimming.

4 my grandparents _____ (visit) us.

Often, …

5 I _____ (go) cycling.

6 it _____ (rain).

Now, …

7 it _____ (rain).

8 my sister _____ (have) a tennis lesson.

Twice a month, …

9 my mum _____ (drive) to London.

10 we _____ (have) football practice.

3 ⭐⭐ **Complete the text with the correct form of the verbs in brackets.**

Bradley Wiggins is an amazing cyclist. He [1]_loves_ (love) cycling and he [2]_____ (train) every day. He [3]_____ (speak) French and he [4]_____ (like) music. He [5]_____ (play) the guitar and he [6]_____ (listen) to old music from the 1960s.

In this photo, Bradley [7]_____ (not cycle). He [8]_____ (not listen) to music and he [9]_____ (not play) the guitar. The sun [10]_____ (shine) and he [11]_____ (sit) outside. He [12]_____ (read) and he is very happy.

4 ⭐⭐⭐ **Write questions.**

1 A: What/your dad/do?

   What does your dad do?

B: He's a doctor.

A: What/he do/at the moment?

   What's he doing at the moment?

B: He's watching television.

2 A: What/your mum/do?

_____

B: She's a teacher?

A: she/teach/now?

_____

B: No, she isn't. She's shopping.

3 A: What/your brother/do/at the moment?

_____

B: He's playing football.

A: he/often/play football?

_____

B: Yes, he does.

4 A: When/you usually/do your homework?

_____

B: I usually do it in the evening.

A: you/do/your homework at the moment?

_____

B: Yes, I am. I've got a lot of homework today.

5 A: your mum/often cook?

_____

B: Yes, she does.

A: she/cook/now?

_____

B: No, she isn't. She's getting pizzas.

Grammar: *Like + -ing*

5 ⭐ **Complete the sentences with the correct form of the verbs in brackets.**

1 I like <u>watching</u> (watch) rugby, but I don't like _____ (play) it.

2 I love _____ (eat), but I hate _____ (cook).

3 I like _____ (go) to school, but I don't like _____ (do) homework.

4 Do you like _____ (swim)?

5 I hate _____ (work), but I like _____ (get) money every week.

6 What do you like _____ (do) at the weekend?

7 My brother likes _____ (surf) the internet, but he doesn't like (windsurf) _____.

8 My sister loves _____ (talk) on the phone, but she doesn't like _____ (write) emails.

Grammar summary

Present simple and present continuous

I usually **work** on Fridays, but I**'m not working** today.

He **doesn't** often **eat** burgers, but he**'s eating** one now.

We **have** tests every week and we**'re having** one at the moment.

Note

Use

- We use the present simple with: adverbs of frequency (*always, never*, etc.) and adverbial phrases of frequency (*every day, twice a week*).
  I **get up** at seven o'clock **every day**.
  My sister **is always** late for school.
- We also use the present simple for things which are always true or facts.
  I **speak** French.
  We **come from** Ireland.
- We use the present continuous with: *now, at the moment, today, this week*, etc.
  I**'m reading at the moment**.
  My dad**'s working today**.

Like + *-ing*

I **like skiing**.
I **hate getting** up.
I **don't like playing** football.

Note

- We use *like/love/hate/don't like* + verb + *-ing* to talk about likes and dislikes.
- We can also follow *like/love/hate/don't like* with a noun.
  I **like playing** football. (I like football.)
  I **hate going** to school. (I hate school.)

Common mistakes.

~~I like cook~~. ✗
I **like cooking**. ✓
~~What do you do at the moment?~~ ✗
What **are you doing** at the moment? ✓
~~I'm like swimming~~. ✗
I **like swimming**. ✓

7c Can you sing?

Vocabulary: Verbs of ability

1 ⭐ **Match the verbs from the box with the activities.**

> • take • make • sew on
> • cook • use • play • ~~ride~~
> • run • send

1 *ride* a horse.
2 _____ a sculpture
3 _____ an email
4 _____ a button
5 _____ photographs
6 _____ a washing machine
7 _____ basketball
8 _____ five kilometres
9 _____ a meal

2 ⭐⭐ **Complete the activities.**

1 Helen is at a disco. She's
   d*ancing*.
2 Tom is at the swimming pool.
   He's d_____ into the water.
3 Our two children have got
   coloured pencils and paper.
   They're d_____.
4 Frank is p_____ a beautiful
   picture of the sea.
5 Cathy is s_____ a Lady
   Gaga song. She's a good singer.
6 Paula and Jane are in the sea.
   They're s_____. They can
   swim very well.
7 David's band are playing in a
   concert. He's p_____ the
   guitar.
8 Emily is doing her homework.
   She's u_____ her computer
   because she's writing a project.

Grammar: Can (ability) Adverb: (not) very well

3 ⭐ **Complete the sentences with the positive and negative forms of *can* and the correct form of the verb in brackets.**

1 I *can swim* (✓ swim), but I *can't ski* (✗ ski).
2 I _____ (✓ cook Italian food),
   but I _____ (✗ cook Chinese
   food).
3 My dad _____ (✓ sew on a
   button), but he _____ (✗ use
   the washing machine).
4 My friend _____ (✓ speak
   Japanese), but he _____
   (✗ read Japanese).
5 I _____ (✗ paint) and I
   _____ (✗ draw).
6 My brother _____ (✓ play the
   guitar), but he _____ (✗ sing).
7 I _____ (✓ cycle), but I
   _____ (✗ ride a horse).
8 My mum _____ (✗ use a
   computer), but she _____
   (✓ take great photos).

4 ⭐⭐ **Complete the dialogues with the correct form of *can* and the words in brackets.**

> **Practical person needed to help in the house. £5 an hour.**

A: Good morning, I'm interested in the job.
B: ¹(sew on a button?)
   Can you sew on a button?
A: ² _____(✓)
B: ³ _____(drive?)
A: ⁴ _____(✗)
B: ⁵ _____(cook?)
A: ⁶ _____(✓, not very well)
B: ⁷ _____(use a washing machine?)
A: ⁸ _____(✓)

Use your English: Make and respond to suggestions

5 ⭐ **Choose the correct answers.**

1 How about ___ swimming?

   a) go   b) going   c) we go

2 Let's ___ a DVD.

   a) watching   b) we watch   c) watch

3 Why don't ___ a drink?

   a) have   b) we have   c) having

4 What about ___ a computer game?

   a) playing   b) we play   c) play

5 Why don't ___ a cake?

   a) make   b) making   c) we make

6 Let's ___ our bedrooms.

   a) tidy   b) we tidy   c) tidying

6 ⭐⭐ **Complete the dialogue with the words from the box.**

> • about • What • ~~why~~ • Great • sure
> • idea • not • Let's

Mia: I'm bored.

Danielle: [1]_Why_ don't we go shopping?

Mia: That's a good [2]_____. I want a new T-shirt.

Danielle: [3]_____ cycle.

Mia: I'm not [4]_____. It's very cloudy. How [5]_____ going by bus?

Danielle: No, [6]_____ today. I hate going by bus on Saturday afternoon. I know! We can phone Tom. He's got a car.

Mia: [7]_____ idea! [8]_____ about asking Vicky? She likes Tom!

Danielle: OK. What's her phone number?

Grammar summary

Can (ability) Adverb: *(not) very well*	
Affirmative	**Negative**
I **can play** tennis.	I **can't play** tennis.
You **can speak** English.	You **can't speak** English.
He **can dance**.	He **can't dance**.
She **can sing**.	She **can't sing**.
We **can draw**.	We **can't draw**.
They **can drive**.	They **can't drive**.
I **can speak** English **very well**.	I **can't speak** English **very well**.
Questions	**Short answers**
Can you **cook**?	Yes, I **can**./No, I **can't**.
Can I **sing**?	Yes, you **can**./No, you **can't**.
Can he **dive**?	Yes, he **can**./No, he **can't**.
Can she **paint**?	Yes, she **can**./No, she **can't**.
Can we **use** a computer?	Yes, we **can**./No, we **can't**.
Can they **speak** French?	Yes, they **can**./No, they **can't**.

Note

Can (ability)

Use

- We use *can* + infinitive to talk about something we are able to do.

Form

- In negative sentences, we add *not* to can (*cannot*). We use *can't* more often than *cannot*.

Common mistakes

~~I can to swim.~~ ✗
I **can swim**. ✓
~~He can drawing.~~ ✗
He **can draw**. ✓
~~Do you can cook?~~ ✗
Can you **cook**? ✓

Adverb: *(not) very well*

- We use *very well* to say that we are very good at something. We add this after the verb.
  I **can** swim **very well**. (= I am very good at swimming.)
- We use *not very well* to say that we can do something, but we are not good at it.
  I **can't** speak English **very well**. (= I can speak a little bit of English, but I am not good at it.)

7 Language round-up

1 Use the verbs in brackets to say what the people are and aren't doing.

1 The man (✗ swim) (dive)

   isn't swimming. He's diving.

2 The sun (✗ shine) (rain)

   _____.

3 The girl (✗ ride) (ride/a bike)

   _____ a horse. _____.

4 The boys (✗ play) (play/volleyball)

   _____ football. _____.

5 The boy (✗ eat) (eat/ice cream) _____

   a burger. _____.

6 The woman (✗ talk) (write/a postcard)

   _____ on the phone. _____.

7 The boy and girl (✗ look) (read) _____

   at the sea. _____.

.../12

2 Complete the text with the correct form of the words in brackets.

Robert Pattinson ★ ★ ★ ★   **STAR FACTS**

Robert Pattinson is famous for the *Twilight* films. He likes ¹_acting_ (act) and he ²_____ (make) a new film at the moment. But, sometimes, he doesn't like ³_____ (be) famous. So, what ⁴_____ (he/do) in his free time?
Robert loves music and he can ⁵_____ (play) the piano and the guitar very ⁶_____ (good). He can also rap! In his free time, he ⁷_____ (play) in a band. Their name is Bad Girl. He ⁸_____ (like) football, but he ⁹_____ (can) play it very well. He ¹⁰_____ (not like) playing any other sports.
He likes ¹¹_____ (hang) out with friends, but he doesn't like people ¹²_____ (call) him RPatz.

.../11

3 Complete the dialogue with the correct form of the words from the box.

• can (x2) • go • look • <s>do</s> (x2)
• not like (x2) • take (x2) • good • play (x3)
• watch • love • wind

Heather: Where's Ian?

Cynthia: He's at school.

Heather: On a Saturday? ¹What *'s* he *doing*?

Cynthia: ²He _____ rugby.

Heather: Oh, of course. He always ³_____ rugby on Saturdays. He's in the school team.

Cynthia: That's right. He ⁴_____ sports. Football, basketball, volleyball, tennis and he can ⁵_____ them all really ⁶_____.

Heather: I know. It isn't fair. I ⁷_____ play any sports well. I like ⁸_____ them on the television, but I ⁹_____ playing them.

Cynthia: What about ¹⁰_____ to watch him today?

Heather: OK. Why ¹¹_____ we cycle?

Cynthia: No. It's very ¹²_____. Let's go by bus.

Heather: Good idea. Where's my camera?

Cynthia: Your camera?

Heather: Yes. We can ¹³_____ some photos of Ian. I love ¹⁴_____ photos.

Cynthia: No! Ian ¹⁵_____ people taking his photo. Come on, hurry up. What ¹⁶_____ you _____ now?

Heather: I ¹⁷_____ for my shoes. I ¹⁸_____ find them. Where are they?

.../17

🎧 11 **LISTEN AND CHECK YOUR SCORE**

Total	.../40

7 Skills practice

SKILLS FOCUS: READING AND WRITING

Read

1 **Read the text quickly and find which of these ideas isn't mentioned.**

Going on a boat

Going to a museum

Going rollerblading

FREE LONDON

London is an expensive city, but you can have fun there for free. Here are some of your ideas. A lot of the museums are free. Go to the Science Museum in South Kensington. Listen to talks, play games and learn. It's amazing. *Jackie*

I love window shopping in London. My favourite shop is Fortnum and Mason's. It's got a lot of beautiful things inside. It's on Piccadilly. That's a famous street. Piccadilly, Regent Street and Oxford Street are all great for shopping. You can sit and read in some of the bookshops and play games in Hamley's. *Erica*

My favourite place is the South Bank, where the London Eye is. I don't go on the Eye because it's expensive. I usually go rollerblading because there aren't any cars. You can often see people playing music or dancing there. Some of them can dance really well. *Gary*

2 **Read the text again and answer the questions.**

1 Where is the Science Museum?

In South Kensington

2 Find three things you can do in the Science Museum.

_____

3 What street is Fortnum and Mason's in?

_____

4 Name two other streets which have got a lot of nice shops in them.

_____

5 Why is the South Bank a good place for rollerblading?

_____

Write

3 **Rewrite the letter correctly.**

Hi Sue,

I'm on holliday in Spain. Its great. There is a lot of nice beaches here and always it is sunny. I going swimming every day. My dad don't go to the beach. He hates sit in the sun. He swim in the hotels swimming pool. The hotel is very modern. There's a big restrant. We have breakfast and dinner there every day. I love Spain food. The fisch is fantastic.

See you soon

Love

Tessa ♥

C— *Tessa, there are a lot of mistakes in this homework. Please write it again.*

Hi Sue,
I'm on holiday …

4 **Look at the notes and write a postcard to a friend.**

You are camping with your parents by the sea in Portugal.

You like the holiday very much.

The weather is good – sunny every day.

You swim in the lake every day, you play volleyball with other children there.

You have barbecues every day.

Your parents go jogging – you don't – don't like it.

Evenings – concerts and dancing – good fun.

Go to bed about twelve o'clock every day!

Hi Tim,
I'm on a camping holiday with my parents in Portugal …

8a I was at home all evening.

Vocabulary: Past adverbial phrases

1 ⬛⭐ **Rewrite the <u>underlined</u> phrases. Use a past adverbial phrase with the same meaning as the underlined words.**

It's a Thursday evening in September and I'm in my 8th year of school.

1 <u>On Wednesday</u>, I was late for school.
   Yesterday, I was late for school.

2 <u>On Wednesday in the afternoon</u>, I was at my friend's house.
   _____, I was at my friend's house.

3 <u>On Wednesday from 6 p.m. to 9 p.m.</u>, I was at the cinema.
   _____, I was at the cinema.

4 <u>On Wednesday from 10 p.m. to 6 a.m. on Thursday morning</u>, my dad was at work.
   _____, my dad was at work.

5 <u>Today, in the morning</u>, I was in an English lesson.
   _____, I was in an English lesson.

6 <u>On Saturday and Sunday</u>, I was at my grandparents' house.
   _____, I was at my grandparents' house.

7 <u>On Friday</u>, I was at a party.
   _____, I was at a party.

8 <u>In August</u>, I was in Spain.
   _____, I was in Spain.

9 <u>In Year 7</u>, I was at a different school.
   _____, I was at a different school.

Grammar: Past simple *to be*

2 ⬛⭐ **Complete the sentences with *was*, *were*, *wasn't* or *weren't*.**

> Monday: at home in bed all day.
> Tuesday: p.m. drama club
> evening: concert with Abi
> Wednesday: late for school ☹
> Thursday: evening — party at my aunt's house.
> Friday: cinema with David — no Tina?? Why not??
> Saturday: London with my parents
> evening: 'Romeo and Juliet' at the Globe Theatre — brilliant!

Hi Tina,

How are you? I'm OK. I ¹*wasn't* OK on Monday. I ² _____ at home in bed all day. On Tuesday, I ³ _____ at school and, in the afternoon, I ⁴ _____ at the drama club. In the evening, Abi and I ⁵ _____ at a concert, but it ⁶ _____ terrible!!

After the concert, I ⁷ _____ tired and, on Wednesday, I ⁸ _____ late for school. On Thursday evening, my mum and I ⁹ _____ at a party at my aunt's house. It ¹⁰ _____ great. My cousins ¹¹ _____ there. They're cool. On Friday evening, I ¹² _____ at the cinema with David, but you ¹³ _____ there. Where ¹⁴ _____ you??

I ¹⁵ _____ in London at the weekend with my parents. The hotel ¹⁶ _____ nice and the shops ¹⁷ _____ fantastic. On Saturday evening, we ¹⁸ _____ at the Globe Theatre to see *Romeo and Juliet*. It ¹⁹ _____ brilliant! All the actors ²⁰ _____ great. Romeo was very good looking!!

See you soon
Simone

3 ★★ Write questions.

1 Where/you/yesterday?

Where were you yesterday?

2 Where/Mark/last Friday?

_____

3 Where/your parents/last weekend?

_____

4 you/late for school yesterday?

_____

5 Amy/at the party last Friday?

_____

6 the concert good?

_____

4 ★★★★ Write questions and answers.

1 A: you/at the cinema /last Friday?

B: ✗ theatre

A: Were you at the cinema last Friday?

B: No, I wasn't. I was at the theatre.

2 A: your sister/at school yesterday?

B: ✗ doctor's

A: _____

B: _____

3 A: your parents/at a music festival last month

B: ✓

A: _____

B: _____

4 A: Where/you/yesterday?

B: /home

A: _____

B: _____

5 A: What/weather like/in Spain?

B: /great!

A: _____

B: _____

6 A: /the scout camp good?

B: ✓ The people there/really nice

A: _____

B: _____

Grammar summary

Past simple of *to be*

Affirmative	Negative
I **was** at home.	I **wasn't** at home.
You **were** late.	You **weren't** late.
He **was** in bed.	He **wasn't** in bed.
She **was** hungry.	She **wasn't** hungry.
It **was** cold.	It **wasn't** cold.
We **were** tired.	We **weren't** tired.
They **were** brilliant.	They **weren't** brilliant.
Questions	Short answers
Were you a scout?	Yes, I **was**./No, I **wasn't**.
Was I correct?	Yes, you **were**./No, you **weren't**.
Was he funny?	Yes, he **was**./No, he **wasn't**.
Was she serious?	Yes, she **was**./No, she **wasn't**.
Was it sunny?	Yes, it **was**./No, it **wasn't**.
Were we late?	Yes, we **were**./No we **weren't**.
Were they famous?	Yes, they **were**./No, they **weren't**.

Note

Use

- We use the past simple of *to be* to talk about the past.
*I **was** at school yesterday.*

Form

- There are two forms in the affirmative: *was* and *were*.
*I/He/She/It **was** funny.*
*We/You/They **were** late.*

Common mistakes

~~You was late.~~ ✗
You **were** late. ✓
~~Where she was?~~ ✗
Where **was** she. ✓

8b They noticed a large animal.

Vocabulary: Years

1 ⭐ **Complete the dates.**

> • 2012 • 1654 • 2005 • 1066 • 1565
> • ~~1789~~ • 1938 • 1492

1 *seventeen* eighty-nine

2 sixteen _____

3 _____ and five

4 _____ thirty-eight

5 twenty_____

6 _____ sixty-five

7 fourteen_____

8 _____ sixty-six

Grammar: Past simple of regular verbs: affirmative and negative

2 ⭐ **Complete the story with the correct form of the verbs in brackets.**

It was ten o'clock at night and dark. Dan and I were on our way home from the cinema. Suddenly, Dan ¹*stopped* (stop). 'Was that a cat?' he ² _____ (ask). 'Where?'

'There. It ³_____ (walk) past that house. It was really big.'

I was cold and tired. I ⁴_____ (want) to go home, but Dan didn't. Dan ⁵_____ (follow) the cat to a small, dark, street.

'Wait!'

Dan ⁶_____ (laugh). 'Are you frightened? Look, I think the cat ⁷_____ (climb) up here. Let's go after it.

'No way!'

I ⁸_____ (watch) Dan start to climb. Suddenly the cat ⁹_____ (jump) onto his head! It was very big and very angry.

'Aaaagh'

Now, I ¹⁰_____ (start) to laugh. 'Dan, are you frightened?!'

We ¹¹_____ (walk) home. Dan ¹²_____ (not talk) to me at all.

3 ⭐⭐ **Make the sentences negative.**

1 We finished the exam at eleven o'clock.
   We didn't finish the exam at eleven o'clock.

2 We talked for five minutes.
   _____

3 I played tennis with my friend.
   _____

4 The train arrived at half past ten.
   _____

5 I realised what it was.
   _____

6 My dad cooked dinner.
   _____

7 Elaine waited for me.
   _____

8 I cycled to school yesterday.
   _____

4 ⭐⭐⭐ **Write sentences.**

1 I/not cook/dinner yesterday. My mum/cook dinner and my dad/help/her
   I didn't cook dinner yesterday. My mum cooked dinner and my dad helped her.

2 You/not tidy/your room. I/ask/you yesterday to tidy it.
   _____
   _____

3 I/not talk/to you yesterday because I/not notice/you.
   _____
   _____

4 We/walk/to school yesterday. We/arrive/late and Mrs Jones/stop/us and/ask/us our names.
   _____
   _____

Grammar: Prepositions of motion

5 ⭐ **Match the actions (1–7) in the picture to prepositions of motion in the box.**

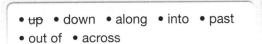

- up • down • along • into • past
- out of • across

1 _up_   5 _____

2 _____   6 _____

3 _____   7 _____

4 _____

Grammar summary

Past simple of regular verbs: *affirmative and negative*	
Affirmative	**Negative**
I **talked** to Stephen.	I **didn't talk** to Stephen.
You **walked** to school.	You **didn't walk** to school.
He **played** football.	He **didn't play** football.
She **waited** for me.	She **didn't wait** for me.
We **tried** to ski.	We **didn't try** to ski.
They **wanted** to go home.	They **didn't want** to go home.

Note

Use

- We use the past simple to talk about actions and situations that started and finished in the past.

Form

- For the past simple affirmative of most regular verbs, we add -*ed*.
  look – looked, watch – watched
- We use the auxiliary *didn't* + infinitive without *to* for negatives.
  stopped – didn't stop, waited – didn't wait

Common mistakes

~~I did phone my friend.~~ ✗
I **phoned** my friend. ✓
~~He didn't wanted to go.~~ ✗
He **didn't want** to go. ✓

Spelling rules

- When a verb ends in -*e*, we just add -*d*.
  like – liked
- When a verb ends in one vowel and one consonant, we usually double the last consonant.
  stop – stopped
- When a verb ends in a consonant + -*y*, the -*y* changes to -*ie* and we add -*d*. We don't change -*y* to -*ie* after a vowel.
  try – tried
  play – played

8c When did this happen?

Grammar: Past simple of regular verbs: questions and short answers

1 ⭐ **Complete the questions and answers with the correct form of the verb in capitals.**

1 PLAY

   A: I _played_ a sport last night.

   B: What sport did you _play_?

2 START

   A: When did the lesson _____?

   B: It _____ at ten o'clock.

3 FINISH

   A: You're late home.

   B: Yes, the film _____ late.

   A: What time did it _____?

4 TALK

   A: I _____ to Katie on the phone last night. My parents were really angry.

   B: Why? How long did you _____ for?

5 WALK

   A: Did you _____ home yesterday?

   B: Well, I _____ from school to my mum's work. I didn't _____ all the way.

6 COOK

   A: Did your dad _____ this dinner?

   B: No. My mum _____ this. My dad can't cook.

2 ⭐⭐ **Match the answers to the questions.**

1 Did you revise for the exam? _d_

2 What time did the bus arrive? __

3 How many questions did you answer in the test? __

4 Did you and your friends watch the James Bond DVD? __

5 Did your mum and dad dance at the party? __

6 Where did you cycle to? __

7 Did your mum sew on that button for you? __

8 Did it rain when you were on holiday? __

a) At 6 p.m.

b) Yes, they did.

c) No, it didn't.

d) Yes, I did.

e) To the river.

f) Yes, she did.

g) Three.

h) No, we didn't.

3 ⭐⭐⭐ **Write questions and answers.**

A: [1]_Did you watch_ (you/watch) the film on television last night?

B: [2]_____ (No/not).

   [3]_____ (I/paint) my bedroom.

A: Wow! [4]_____ (What colour/you/paint) it?

B: Green.

A: [5]_____ (you/play) your new computer game last night?

B: [6]_____ (Yes/do).

A: [7]_____ (What time/you finish) playing?

B: At about 1 a.m. I'm really tired now.

Vocabulary: Adjectives of feeling

4 ★ **Choose the correct options.**

1 I've got an important exam tomorrow.
  a) I'm bored. b) I'm worried. c) I'm angry.

2 The summer holidays start tomorrow.
  a) I'm fed up   b) I'm scared.   c) I'm happy.

3 My friends are going to the cinema, but they didn't ask me.
  a) I'm tired.   b) I'm excited.   c) I'm fed up.

4 There's nothing to do.
  a) I'm bored.   b) I'm worried.   c) I'm scared.

5 I'm going to see my favourite band in concert.
  a) I'm worried. b) I'm excited. c) I'm bored.

6 I played computer games until 4 a.m.
  a) I'm bored.   b) I'm sad.   c) I'm tired.

Use your English: Ask about problems

5 ★ **Complete the dialogue with the words from the box.**

• mind • just • problem • don't • ~~matter~~ • bit

A: Hi, Tom. What's the ¹*matter*?
B: Nothing. I'm ²_____ a ³_____ fed up.
A: Why? What's the ⁴_____?
B: Tricia doesn't want to talk to me. She didn't phone me yesterday.
A: Never ⁵_____. Why ⁶_____ you phone her?
B: I tried, but she didn't answer.

6 ★★ **Number the conversation in the correct order.**

☐ a) Well, no. Not really. I'm angry with Tom.

☐ b) Never mind. I'm sure he's sorry.

☐ c) Yes, I'm sure. Why don't you phone him and talk to him?

1 d) Hi, Shelly. Can I talk to you?

☐ e) Nothing, I'm fine.

☐ f) Oh dear. Why are you angry?

☐ g) Do you think so?

☐ h) Hi Tricia. Of course. What's the problem?

☐ i) Because he laughed at my new hat.

☐ j) Really?

Grammar summary

Past simple of regular verbs: questions and short answers	
Questions	**Short answers**
Did you **watch** the film?	Yes, I **did**./No, I **didn't**.
Did I **finish**?	Yes, you **did**./No, you **didn't**.
Did he **notice** us?	Yes, he **did**./No, he **didn't**.
Did she **talk** to you?	Yes, she **did**./No, she **didn't**.
Did it **rain**?	Yes, it **did**./No, it **didn't**.
Did we **start**?	Yes, we **did**./No, we **didn't**.
Did they **phone** you?	Yes, they **did**./No, they **didn't**.

Note

Form

• In questions, the word order is (Question word) + *Did* + subject + infinitive without *to*.
  ***Where did you go** last night?*
  ***What did you do** yesterday?*

• In short responses we use the auxiliaries *did/didn't*. We don't use the main verb.
  ***Did** you **like** the film? Yes, I **did**. NOT ~~Yes, I liked.~~*

Common mistakes

~~Did you revised?~~ ✗
Did you **revise**? ✓
~~It rained?~~ ✗
Did it **rain**? ✓

8 Language round-up

1 Complete the text about Allison Miller with the correct forms of the verbs from the box.

> • move (x2) • want • study • ~~not be~~ • start
> • not stay • notice • be (x2)

Allison Miller is an American actress, but she
[1]*wasn't* born in America. She [2]_____
born in Italy, but she [3]_____ there. Her
family [4]_____ back to the USA when she
[5]_____ young.
Allison is very clever and she [6]_____ at the
University of Florida, but she really [7]_____
to be an actress. She [8]_____ her acting
career in Florida and, in 2006, she [9]_____ to
Hollywood. Film makers soon [10]_____ her
and she is now a young star of television and film.

…/9

2 Complete the text with one word or contraction in each space.

[1]<u>Last</u> Saturday, I was [2]b_____ because
there was nothing to do so I walked to my friend's
house. We [3]w_____ a DVD and then our
friend Sandra phoned and [4]a_____ us to
meet her in a café. It [5]w_____ a nice day
so we [6]w_____ into town.
We walked [7]a_____ the river for one
kilometre, [8]p_____ the cinema and, when
the cars stopped, [9]a_____ the big road in
the town centre. We walked [10]i_____ the
café, but Sandra [11]w_____ there.
We tried to phone her, but there was no answer.
On Monday, we [12]w_____ angry with her,
but she was very surprised. 'I [13]d_____
phone you,' she said. 'I was at my aunt's house.
My phone was in my bedroom at home. My
little sister was at home and …' She suddenly
[14]s_____ talking and started laughing. We
[15]l_____, too. Her sister. Her annoying little
sister. It was her!

…/14

3 Write questions and answers.

A: Luke/be/bored/night?
A: [1]<u>*Was Luke bored last night?*</u>
B: [2]_____ ✓
A: you/watch/TV/night?
A: [3]_____
B: [4]_____ ✗
A: What/matter?   B: I/bit/fed up.
A: [5]_____
B: [6]_____
A: What games/you/play/last weekend?
A: [7]_____
B: I/not/play any games.
B: [8]_____
A: your mum/like present?   B: ✓ She/love/it.
A: [9]_____
B: [10]_____

…/9

4 Choose the correct answers.

1 ___ you finish your work yesterday?
  a) Were   b) Do   c) Did
2 What time did you ___ me?
  a) phone   b) phoning   c) phoned
3 I was ___ bed when my friend arrived.
  a) at   b) on   c) in
4 We walked out ___ the room.
  a) of   b) from   c) off
5 'I failed my exams.' 'Never ___.'
  a) matter   b) worry   c) mind
6 I'm ___. There's nothing to do.
  a) excited   b) tired   c) bored
7 Where ___ yesterday?
  a) did you   b) were you c) you were
8 I phoned Dan ___ night.
  a) yesterday b) past   c) last
9 Why ___ you phone your friends?
  a) does   b) don't   c) aren't

…/8

🔊 12	**LISTEN AND CHECK YOUR SCORE**
Total	…/40

8 Skills practice

SKILLS FOCUS: READING, LISTENING AND WRITING

Read

1 **Read the text quickly and choose the best title.**

A I don't like the activities at my school.

B I'm having problems with my exams.

C I can only do one of my favourite activities.

Can you help me? I don't know what to do. I'm in Year 9 of school and I love drama and football. This year is a difficult year because we've got a lot of important exams in June. Last year, I was in the school play. It was great fun. Often, I didn't finish my homework until midnight because I wanted to learn my lines. Some weeks, I didn't use my computer at all!

Now, I'm in the school football team. We have football practice on Tuesdays and Thursdays. My best friends are in the team. The problem is that drama club rehearsals are on Tuesdays and Thursdays, too. I want to go to both, but I can't. My parents don't want me to be in the play because learning lines is difficult. My friends want me to play football. Last Tuesday I played football, but I missed drama club and on Thursday I was at the play rehearsal. Now my friends, my PE teacher and my Drama teacher are all angry with me. So, what do I do?

2 **Read the text again and answer true (T) or false (F).**

1 The writer is in Year 8 at school. _F_

2 He has got important exams in May.

3 Last year, he was in the school play.

4 Often, he didn't arrive home until midnight.

5 He has football practice twice a week.

6 His best friends go to drama club.

7 Drama club is on Tuesdays and Thursdays.

8 His parents are angry with him.

Listen

3 🔊13 **Look at the pictures. Then listen to a conversation and complete the sentences.**

1 Olivia is feeling _fed_ up.

2 She dropped her _____.

3 It happened at school, in Room _____, at _____ time.

4 Alina wasn't at the quiz because she was at a _____.

5 Billy Davies pushed Alina off the bus last _____.

6 Alina's idea is to ask Mr Simmons because he is very _____.

7 Olivia thinks it is a _____ idea.

Write

4 **Answer the questions to make a blog about what happened yesterday.**

A friend phoned you? Who? When? Why?

1 _Yesterday, at nine o'clock, Maria phoned me._
She wanted to play tennis.

You didn't want to play tennis. Why not?

2 _____

You wanted to watch a DVD. Which DVD?

3 _____

Where did you watch the DVD? Did Maria like it?

4 _____

Suddenly someone knocked on the door. Who was it? What did he/she want?

5 _____

9a They went to New York.

Grammar: Past simple of irregular verbs: affirmative and negative

1 ★ Complete the past simple form of the verbs.

1 come   c a m e
2 go   __ e __ __
3 buy   b __ __ __ __ __
4 drive   d __ __ __ e
5 write   __ __ __ t __
6 sleep   __ l __ __ __
7 say   s __ __ __
8 make   __ a __ __
9 ride   r __ __ __
10 have   __ a __

2 ★★ Complete the sentences with the correct form of the verbs.

1 My brother _sold_ (sell) his camera last week.

2 My dad _____ (go) to London last week, but he _____ (not drive). He _____ (go) by train.

3 My girlfriend _____ (buy) me this book for my birthday, but I _____ (not buy) her a present. I _____ (forget) her birthday.

4 I'm tired. I _____ (not sleep) all night.

5 Ian Fleming _____ (not write) the Jason Bourne books. He _____ (write) the James Bond books.

6 I _____ (have) a great holiday. I _____ (ride) a horse and _____ (meet) some cool people.

7 I _____ (go) to the cinema last night, but I _____ (not see) a film. I waited for my friends there.

8 Macbeth _____ (not say) 'To be or not to be?'. Hamlet _____ (say) it.

3 ★★★ Complete the text using the correct form of the verbs in brackets.

In 1934, Theresa Wallach and Florence Blenkiron travelled together from London to Cape Town in South Africa. They [1]_didn't go_ (not go) by plane, they [2]_____ (not drive) a car. They [3]_____ (ride) on a motorbike. They [4]_____ (not have) any help. There weren't any people with them. On the way, they [5]_____ (have) a lot of problems, but they [6]_____ (meet) friendly people and, in the end, arrived in South Africa. After the journey, they were famous and Wallach [7]_____ (write) their story in the book _The Rugged Road_. After the Second World War, Wallach [8]_____ (go) to the USA and [9]_____(ride) a motorbike around the country for two and a half years. In 1952, she moved to the USA to live and work. She [10]_____ (have) a motorbike shop there. One day, in 1959, three men [11]_____ (come) into the shop to buy motorbikes for a holiday in Europe. She [12]_____ (not sell) them bikes because she was worried about them. She gave them lessons about motorbike riding and, when they were ready, they [13]_____ (buy) the bikes and [14]_____ (have) a great holiday in Europe. That's when Theresa realised she was a good teacher. She [15]_____ (write) another book, _Easy Motorbike Riding_, [16]_____ (sell) her shop and opened a school; The Easy Riding Academy. She really was an amazing woman and she lived to the age of 90, a lover of motorbikes until the end.

Vocabulary: Transport

4 ⭐ **Label the pictures with the words from the box.**

> • scooter • ~~taxi~~ • plane • underground
> • boat • train • coach • lorry • bike

1 _taxi_

2 _____

3 _____

4 _____

5 _____

6 _____

7 _____

8 _____

9 _____

Grammar: *By + means of transport*

5 ⭐ **Complete the text with one word in each space.**

> Hi Max,
>
> I'm in Greece. We came here ¹*by plane*.
>
> The journey was fine. Then we went
>
> ² _____ _____ to Piraeus and
>
> we went to Aegina ³ _____
>
> _____.
>
> It was 1 km to our hotel. We wanted to go
>
> ⁴ _____ _____, but we
>
> didn't see one so we went
>
> ⁵ _____ _____. It was very hot.
>
> Now we go to beaches and other places
>
> ⁶ _____ _____. It's great.
>
> See you soon
>
> Love
>
> *Tracey*

Grammar summary

Past simple of irregular verbs: *affirmative and negative*

Affirmative	Negative
I **went** to Greece.	I **didn't go** to Greece.
You **came** home late.	You **didn't come** home late.
He **drove** to London.	He **didn't drive** to London.
She **bought** a DVD.	She **didn't buy** a DVD.
We **had** a good time.	We **didn't have** a good time.
They **sold** their house.	They **didn't sell** their house.

Note

Form

- Some verbs are irregular and do not form the past simple with *-ed*, for example:

  have – had   do – did
  go – went   buy – bought
  make – made   sleep – slept
  take – took   see – saw

- To make negative sentences, we use *didn't* + infinitive without *to*

  I **didn't meet** my friends last weekend.

Common mistakes

~~She didn't went.~~ ✗
She **didn't go**. ✓
~~I buyed a new computer.~~ ✗
I **bought** a new computer. ✓

by + means of transport

To go/travel …
- **by** bus, car, taxi, train, plane, tram, underground, lorry, boat
- **on** foot

Note

- To answer the question *How did you travel?*, we say:
  *I went / travelled **by** + (bus, car, etc.)*
- But we say *on foot*.
  *I went to the beach **on foot**.*

Common mistakes

~~We went to the shops by foot.~~ ✗
We went to the shops **on foot**. ✓

9b I went to Canada two years ago.

Vocabulary: Landscape

1 ⭐ **Look at the picture and complete the words.**

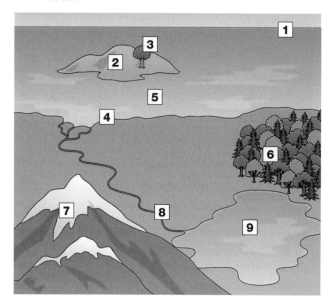

1 o_cean_	6 f_____
2 i_____	7 m_____
3 t_____	8 r_____
4 c_____	9 l_____
5 s_____	

Vocabulary: Holiday activities

2 ⭐ **Match the activities to the people and complete the sentences.**

- go climbing • go shopping
- go swimming • go skiing • go windsurfing
- go to museums • go sunbathing
- go sightseeing • go to the beach

Jack went to Paris in March. He ...

1 _went shopping_   3 _____

2 _____

Elaine went to a small Greek island in the summer. She ...

4 _____   6 _____

5 _____   7 _____

Sammy went to the mountains in the summer and in the winter. He ...

8 _____ in the summer.

9 _____ in the winter.

Grammar: Past simple with *ago*

3 ⭐ **Choose the correct answers.**

1 It's March now. Our skiing holiday was in January. It was ___.
a) one month ago   b) two weeks ago
c) two months ago

2 Lessons are 45 minutes and we finish in fifteen minutes. The lesson started ___.
a) thirty minutes ago
b) forty-five minutes ago
c) fifteen minutes ago

3 I'm fourteen years old. I was born ___.
a) fourteen years ago
b) fourteen months ago
c) fourteen weeks ago

4 The school year started in September. It's now May. Only two months and then it's the holidays. I can't believe that school started ___.
a) two months ago   b) eight months ago
c) one year ago

5 My sister is twelve now. When she was seven, she got a red bike. She got it ___.
a) twelve years ago   b) seven years ago
c) five years ago

6 My birthday was three months ago. Now it's July. My birthday was in ___.
a) July   b) April   c) October

4 ★★★ Read the blog and complete the questions and answers.

> **14/8 4.30 p.m.**
> What a holiday. See our photos on Facebook! We had an awesome time. We left on July 14. We flew to Sicily and then went by taxi to our apartment. It was really beautiful. Here are some of the things we did. More later.
>
> 1/8 Noto – beautiful city
>
> 7/8 Climbed Mount Etna. Incredible. Really cold on top!
>
> 11/8 Went shopping in Taormina. Bought some cool things.
>
> Today 4.30 a.m. – went to the airport
>
> 6.00 a.m. flew to Rome
>
> 10.30 a.m. on the plane to London
>
> 1.30 p.m. arrived in London
>
> 4.00 p.m. HOME
>
> 4.28 p.m. started writing this blog!!

1 When/they leave? (month)

When did they leave?

They left one month ago.

2 When/they go to/Noto? (weeks)

_____

_____

3 When/they climb/Mount Etna? (week)

_____

_____

4 When/they go/shopping in Toarmina? (days)

_____

_____

5 When/they go/to the airport? (hours)

_____

_____

6 When/they arrive/in London? (hours)

_____

_____

7 When/they get/home? (minutes)

_____

_____

8 When/they start/writing the blog? (minutes)

_____

_____

Grammar summary

Past simple with *ago*

I went to France **two years/three months/two weeks ago**.

She arrived home **three hours/ten minutes ago**.

I saw this film **one month/two weeks/two days ago**.

Note

Use

- We use *ago* to say how many weeks, years, months, days, hours, minutes, etc. before now something happened. (It's now 10 p.m. I went to bed at ten minutes to ten.)
  *I went to bed ten minutes **ago**.*

Common mistakes

~~I bought my ticket before three weeks.~~ ✗

~~I bought my ticket three weeks before.~~ ✗

*I bought my ticket three weeks **ago**.* ✓

9c It's opposite the station.

Grammar: Imperatives

1 ⭐ **Complete the imperatives with the verbs from the box.**

- ~~listen~~ • work • not talk • tidy • not eat
- hurry • not look • calm • not be • write

1 *Listen* to your teacher.
2 _____ at me. I don't know the answer.
3 _____ in the test.
4 _____ your name and address here.
5 _____ down!
6 _____ up!
7 _____ my sandwiches.
8 _____ your bedroom.
9 _____ silly.
10 _____ hard.

Vocabulary: Places in town

2 ⭐⭐ **Write the places.**

1 I need some money. I'm going to the *bank*.
2 Mark's at the bus s_____ waiting for a bus.
3 I need some medicine. I'm going to the p_____.
4 I can go to the n_____ if you want a newspaper.
5 Let's go for a walk in the p_____.
6 There's no food in the fridge. Let's go to an Italian r_____ for dinner.
7 We can go to the c_____ for a drink and a cake.
8 Do you want a stamp? I'm going to the p_____ o_____.
9 We can get all our shopping in the big s_____.
10 The train arrives at the s_____ at ten o'clock.

Grammar: Prepositions of place

3 ⭐ **Look at the map and circle the correct answer.**

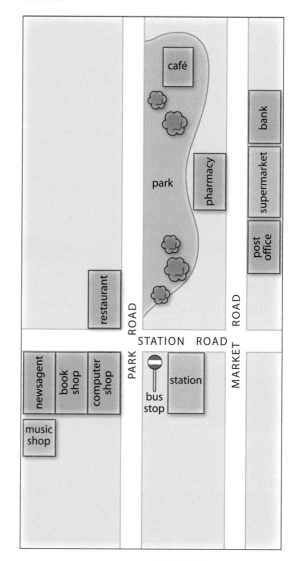

1 The restaurant is **in** / **opposite** / **between** the park.
2 The computer shop is **next to** / **behind** / **under** the book shop.
3 The computer shop is **between** / **in front of** / **on the corner of** Park Road and Station Road.
4 The station is **in** / **opposite** / **behind** Station Road.
5 The bank is **next to** / **near** / **under** the café.
6 The supermarket is **behind** / **between** / **opposite** the post office and the bank.
7 The bus stop is **under** / **in** / **opposite** the computer shop.
8 The pharmacy is **behind** / **in** / **on** the park.

4 ⭐⭐ **Look at the map again and write sentences.**

1 The music shop/the computer shop

   The music shop is near the computer shop.

2 The book shop/the newsagent/the computer shop

   _____

3 The pharmacy/the supermarket

   _____

4 The station/Park Road/Market Road

   _____

5 The restaurant/the corner/Park Road/Station Road

   _____

6 The bus stop/the station

   _____

7 The café/the park

   _____

8 The pharmacy/Market Road

   _____

9 The café/the pharmacy

   _____

Use your English: Ask for help in a town

5 ⭐ **Complete the dialogues with one word in each space.**

1 A: *Excuse* me, where's the bank?

   B: It's _____ Station Road.

   A: Thanks very _____.

2 A: Excuse me, _____ there a post office near here?

   B: Yes, there's _____ in Park Road. It's _____ a café and a bank.

   A: Thank you.

   B: You're _____.

3 A: Excuse me, where's the _____ cashpoint?

   B: I'm _____. I don't _____. I'm not _____ here.

4 A: Excuse me, _____'s the park?

   B: It's opposite the station.

   A: Thank you.

   B: That's _____ right.

Grammar summary

Imperatives	
Affirmative	**Negative**
Come here!	**Don't move!**
Sit down!	**Don't drink** that!

Note

Use

- We use imperatives to tell someone to do something or not to do something.

Form

- We use the infinitive without a subject to make the imperative.
- We use *Don't* + the infinitive to make negative imperatives.
- We can use *please* at the beginning or end of an imperative to make it more polite. **Please** be quiet. Come here, **please**.

Prepositions of place

The bank is **between** the supermarket and the restaurant.
The cinema is **opposite** the station.
The music shop is **near** the bus stop.
The café is **on** the corner of Dale Street and Oxford Road.

1 Rearrange the letters to make words. Write them in the correct columns.

~~mart~~	mgclniib	kingis
iegngeihsst	creosto	socat
liadsn	roebokmit	cchoa
alek	binganutsh	caneo

Transport	**Activities**	**Landscape**
tram	_____	_____
_____	_____	_____
_____	_____	_____
_____	_____	_____

.../11

2 Complete the text with the words from the box.

> • didn't • on • drove • between
> • underground • see • went • ago • ~~had~~
> • by • go • did • how

Danielle: Hi, Donna. I'm back from Europe. We ¹*had* a great time.

Donna: Hi, Danielle. When ²_____ you get back?

Danielle: About three hours ³_____.

Donna: So, tell me all about it.

Danielle: Well, first of all, we ⁴_____ to Paris. We didn't go ⁵_____ plane. My dad ⁶_____. He was a bit frightened by all the other cars!

Donna: ⁷_____ did you travel in Paris?

Danielle: We went by ⁸_____. They call it the metro. Oh and ⁹_____ foot.

Donna: Did you ¹⁰_____ the Mona Lisa?

Danielle: No, I ¹¹_____. We didn't ¹²_____ to the Louvre.

Donna: Where was your hotel?

Danielle: It was ¹³_____ the Arc de Triomphe and the River Seine.

Donna: So, what did you do after Paris?

.../12

3 Complete the email with the correct form of the verbs in brackets.

Hi Ben,

Thanks for the email. I'm sorry I ¹*didn't write* (not write) to you yesterday, but it was my mum's birthday. My sister and I ²_____ (make) a cake and ³_____ (buy) some flowers. My mum ⁴_____ (have) a party in the evening and lots of people ⁵_____ (come). What ⁶_____ (you/do) last night? ⁷_____ (you/meet) your friends? I ⁸_____ (see) Paul in the town centre, but he ⁹_____ (not see) me. Right, It's time for bed. I ¹⁰_____ (not sleep) much last night and I'm tired.
Phil
PS ¹¹_____ (you/buy) the tickets for the concert?

.../10

4 Choose the correct options.

1 We did our sightseeing ___ foot.
   a) by   b) on   c) with

2 Did you go to the beach? Yes, we ___.
   a) did   b) went   c) did go

3 On holiday, we ___ windsurfing every day.
   a) had   b) played   c) went

4 The train arrived ten minutes ___.
   a) past   b) ago   c) behind

5 It was great. I rode on a ___.
   a) car   b) plane   c) motorbike

6 Can you get me some medicine from the ___?
   a) pharmacy   b) café   c) station

7 The restaurant is ___ the corner of Park Road and London Road.
   a) in   b) at   c) on

8 What ___ yesterday?
   a) you did   b) you do   c) did you do

.../7

🎧 14 **LISTEN AND CHECK YOUR SCORE**	
Total	.../40

9 Skills practice

SKILLS FOCUS: READING AND WRITING

Read

1 Read the texts quickly and match the photos to the texts.

A

Come to Krakow. Krakow is a beautiful city and perfect for shopping and sightseeing. You can come by plane, car or train and then use the buses and trams. And it's only two hours by car or train to the mountains where you can go skiing or climbing. Krakow centre is quite small and you can see the old town and castle on foot and, when you get tired, you can stop at a café.

B

Bornholm is a beautiful island in the Baltic Sea. There are forests and great beaches. It's a small island and a lot of people travel around by bike. You can fly to Bornholm or go by boat from Germany, Poland, Sweden or Denmark. It's a great place for swimming and windsurfing.

C

Windermere is in the north of England. It's a great place for walking and, in the summer, you can go across Lake Windermere by boat. You can get to Windermere by train. From the station it's a fifteen-minute walk to the lake.

1

2

3

2 Read the text again and complete the information.

	Activities	Transport
Krakow	¹*Shopping* ²_____	Arrive: plane, ³_____ ⁴_____ See the city: ⁵_____
Bornholm	⁶_____ ⁷_____	Arrive: plane, ⁸_____ See the island: ⁹_____
Windermere	¹⁰_____	Arrive: ¹¹_____ Cross the lake: ¹²_____

Write

3 Complete the email with the words from the box.

• after (x2) • ~~First~~ (x2) • that
• Then (x2)

✕

Hi Stella,

We're in our hotel in Ronda in the south of Spain. It's beautiful, but what a journey!
¹*First* we flew from London to Malaga. ²_____ we took a taxi to the station and waited for the train. We got a train to Marbella. After ³_____, we went to get a car. ⁴_____ a long wait we were ready to go. Of course, everything went wrong. ⁵_____, dad drove on the left and a policeman stopped him. ⁶_____ he went east, back to Malaga! ⁷_____ three hours we arrived in Ronda!
I hope we go on foot tomorrow!!
Best wishes
Katie

---

4 Use the notes to write an email to a friend about a journey.

A bad journey
• the plane was late
• didn't know where to get off the bus. Went past our hotel
• dad left his wallet on the bus
• hotel receptionist helped dad get it back

Hi Rose,
We're in Greece. What a journey!

10a Which tent is the best?

Phrases

1 ⭐ **Complete the dialogue with the words from the box.**

> • see • one • Wait • ~~impossible~~
> • Let • minute

Leader: Put your tent up!

Adam: This is ¹ _impossible_. Can you help me?

Liam: ² _____ me ³ _____. This goes here and that goes ... Where does that go?

Adam: I don't know.

Liam: ⁴ _____ a ⁵ _____. There are some different tents over here. Let's find an easier one. ... Here we are. A one piece, pop-up tent.

Adam: That's the ⁶ _____ for me!

Vocabulary: Short adjectives

2 ⭐ **Complete the opposite adjectives.**

1	good	b_ad_
2	big	s_____
3	clean	d_____
4	hot	c_____
5	easy	h_____
6	far	n_____
7	fast	s_____
8	heavy	l_____
9	short	l_____/t_____
10	old	n_____/y _____

Grammar: Comparative and superlative of short adjectives

3 ⭐ **Complete the sentences using the correct comparative form of the adjectives in brackets.**

Henry	Josh

1 Henry (old) _is older than_ Josh.

2 Josh _____ (young) Henry.

3 Henry _____ (light) Josh.

4 Josh _____ (heavy) Henry.

5 Henry _____ (tall) Josh.

6 Josh _____ (short) Henry.

7 Henry's hair _____ (short) Josh's hair.

8 Josh's hair _____ (long) Henry's hair.

9 Josh's eyes _____ (big) Henry's eyes.

10 Henry's eyes _____ (small) Josh's eyes.

4 ⭐⭐ **Complete the dialogues with the correct form of the adjectives in capitals.**

1 EASY/CHEAP/~~BAD~~

A: Oh no. It's raining. The rain is coming into the tent. This is the _worst_ tent in England! Why did you buy it?

B: It was the _____ tent in the shop and it was the _____ to put up.

2 FAST/GOOD/BIG

A: My dad's got a new car. It's really good.

B: Yes? Is it _____ than his old car?

A: I think so. It's _____ than the old car. It can go at 120 miles an hour.

B: Wow, that's fast.

A: And it's _____ than the old car. We can get five people in this one.

3 HARD/EASY/HARD

A: I hate Maths. I think it's the _____ subject at school.

B: Really? I like Maths. I think French is _____ than Maths. I don't understand French at all.

A: French? French is great. It's _____ than Maths.

5 ★★★ **Look at the information and make sentences.**

	Hotel Belle Vue	Royal Hotel	Seaside Hotel
How much? Room for one night	[1]£50	£120	[2]£89
How far? Distance to the town centre	3 km	[3]2 km	[4]5 km
How big? Number of rooms	[5]12	[6]125	58
How old? Age of hotel	75	[7]21	12
How good? Overall/10	6.5	9.8	[8]8.1

1 The Hotel Belle Vue *is the cheapest*.

2 The Seaside Hotel _____ the Royal Hotel.

3 The Royal Hotel _____ to the town centre.

4 The Seaside Hotel _____ from the town centre.

5 The Hotel Belle Vue _____.

6 The Royal Hotel _____.

7 The Royal Hotel _____ the Seaside Hotel, but it's _____ the Hotel Belle Vue.

8 The Seaside Hotel _____ the Hotel Belle Vue, but it's _____ the Royal Hotel.

Grammar summary

Comparative and superlative of short adjectives
+ -er/-est
*I'm **shorter** than you.* *He's **the tallest** boy in the class.*
+ -y → -ier/-y → -iest
*This tent is **heavier** than that one.* *English is the **easiest** subject at school.*
+ -r/-st
*Meg is **nicer** than her sister.* *The band are singing their **latest** song.*
Double final consonant + -er/-est
*Rome is **hotter** than London.* *Paris is **the biggest** city in France.*
Irregular adjectives: *good, bad, far*
*This is a **better** website than that one.* *What's **the best** film of the year?* *This test was **worse** than the last one.* *Monday is **the worst** day of the week.* *Your house is **farther** from the school than my house.* *Jack's house is **the farthest** from the school.*

Note

Use

• We use comparative adjectives to compare two people or things.

• We use superlative adjectives to compare a person or a thing with more than two people or things.

Spelling rules: adjectives ending in a vowel + -y

We don't change the -*y* when it comes after a vowel.

  *It's **the greyest** day of the year.*

We don't double -*y* or -*w*.

  *This is **the newest** car in the street.*

Common mistakes

~~I'm more faster than you.~~ ✗

I'm **faster than** you. ✓

~~This is the baddest film in the world?~~ ✗

This is **the worst** film in the world. ✓

~~We're older from you.~~ ✗

We're **older than** you. ✓

10b It's more exciting than skiing.

Vocabulary: Adjectives of quality

1 ⭐ **Complete the adjectives.**

1 This book is awful. It's really b <u>o</u> <u>r</u> i n <u>g</u>.

2 It's important to make your project look
a __ __ r __ __ t __ __ __ so that people want
to read it.

3 I don't want to go to school in your brother's
car. He's a very d __ __ g __ __ o __ __ driver.

4 I don't know where to go next summer. Spain
or Italy. It's a d __ __ __ __ c __ __ t choice.

5 Rooms in this hotel are only £15 a night. That's
not e __ p __ __ __ __ v __ at all.

6 I'm glad I'm not f __ m __ __ s. I don't want
people to take my photograph all the time.

7 You're very t __ __ __ n __ __ d. You can sing,
dance and play the guitar.

8 The film was very f __ __ g __ t __ __ __ __ g.
I slept with my light on.

2 ⭐ **Choose the correct options.**

1 Don't go climbing in this weather. It's very ___.
a) dangerous b) attractive c) talented

2 It's ___ to work hard and do well in your exams.
a) interesting b) exciting c) important

3 Skiing is really ___. I love it!
a) useful b) talented c) exciting

4 The book you gave me about Hollywood was
very ___.
a) famous b) interesting c) beautiful

5 English is very ___. It can help you get a job.
a) useful b) exciting c) talented

6 She's very ___, but she isn't a very good
actress.
a) expensive b) beautiful c) difficult

7 Sunday afternoons with nothing to do are
very ___.
a) boring b) attractive c) dangerous

8 I want to be a famous musician, but I'm not
very ___.
a) important b) useful c) talented

Grammar: Comparative and superlative of long adjectives

3 ⭐ **Choose the correct options.**

1 I want to buy the **more expensive** /
most expensive phone in the shop.

2 Smartphones are **more expensive** / **most
expensive** than normal phones, but they are
more useful / **most useful** too.

3 Climbing is **more dangerous** / **most
dangerous** than skiing.

4 What is the **more dangerous** / **most
dangerous** sport?

5 Do you think girls with dark hair are **more
attractive** / **most attractive** than girls with
blonde hair?

6 The **more talented** / **most talented** artist I
know is a boy in our school. He's amazing.

7 That was the **more boring** / **most boring** day
out this year.

8 The theatre is **more interesting** / **most
interesting** than the cinema, but the cinema is
more exciting / **most exciting**.

4 ⭐⭐ **Complete the dialogues with the correct
form of the adjectives in brackets.**

1 A: I'm bored.

B: Why don't you do your homework?

A: That's *more boring* (boring) than doing
nothing.

B: It's _____ (useful) as well.

A: Yes, but I can do it later. Now I want to go
out and play a sport.

B: Sport? Is that the _____
(exciting) thing you can think of? Why
don't you go to a museum? Museums are
_____ (interesting) than
sport.

A: No, sport is the _____
(interesting) activity there is.

2 A: Who's that?

   B: Angelina Jolie.

   A: Who?

   B: You don't know? She's the _____ (famous) actress in Hollywood. Some people say she's the _____ (beautiful), too.

   A: I don't think so. I like Penelope Cruz. I think she's _____ (attractive) than Angelina Jolie.

   B: Well, you may be right. Who do you think the _____ (talented) actress is?

   A: Meryl Streep.

5 ★★★ **Write sentences.**

1 Lady Gaga/famous/Britney Spears

   Lady Gaga is more famous than Britney Spears.

2 Madonna/talented/Lady Gaga

   _____

3 Lady Gaga/famous/singer in the world

   _____

4 Britney Spears/attractive/Lady Gaga

   _____

5 Madonna/not/talented singer I know

   _____

6 talented singer I know/Adele

   _____

7 Madonna's concerts/exciting/Britney Spears' concerts

   _____

8 Madonna's concerts/expensive/Britney Spears' concerts

   _____

9 The Rolling Stones' concerts/expensive/concerts

   _____

Grammar summary

Comparative and superlative of long adjectives

This lesson is **more interesting** than yesterday's lesson.

Windsurfing is **more difficult** than swimming.

The British Museum is **the most interesting** museum in the world.

Seth is **the most talented** musician in our class.

Note

Form

- For comparatives of adjectives of two syllables we use *more + adjective*.
- For superlatives of adjectives of two syllables or more, we use *most + adjective*.
- For adjectives of two syllables ending in *-y*, we usually add *–y* ➝ *ier/-y* ➝ *iest* as for short adjectives.
  pretty – prettier NOT *more pretty*
  heavy – heavier NOT *more heavy*

Common mistakes

~~This book is more boringer than that book~~. ✗

This book is **more boring** than that book. ✓

~~This is the most importantest test of the year.~~ ✗

This is **the most important** test of the year. ✓

10c How are you going to choose?

Vocabulary: Types of music

1 ⭐ **Rearrange the letters to make different kinds of music.**

1 par
  rap

5 antiL
  _____

2 hencot
  _____

6 lissalcca
  _____

3 hayev teaml
  _____

7 ulos
  _____

4 eggear
  _____

8 cork
  _____

2 ⭐⭐ **Choose the correct words.**

1 Not many young people listen to **pop** / **jazz**.

2 Do you like hip-**rap** / **hop**?

3 A lot of people in the USA listen to country and
  techno / **western** music.

4 **Latin** / **Reggae** music comes from Jamaica.

5 We listened to an orchestra playing **classical** / **soul**
  music.

6 Who is your favourite **R & B** / **B & R** singer?

7 There were bands from all over the world playing
  traditional music from their country at the **folk** /
  Latin festival.

Grammar: *Going to* for future plans and intentions

3 ⭐ **Complete the sentences with the correct form of *going to* and the verbs in brackets.**

How to become famous!

1 I _'m going to learn_ (learn) to play the guitar.
2 I _____ (find) three other
  musicians.
3 I_____ (not sing).
4 Mark _____ (be) the
  singer.
5 We _____ (practise) every
  day.
6 We _____ (write) some
  songs.
7 We _____ (not sell) them.
8 We _____ (put) them on
  the internet.
9 We _____ (be) famous but
  we _____ (not be) rich.

Monday:	Write emails
Tuesday:	Go shopping. Buy a present for dad.
Wednesday:	Make a cake with mum
Thursday:	Go to the library with Helen
Friday:	Stay in? Do my homework? NO WAY. Meet my friends? YES!
Saturday:	Get up late!

4 ⭐⭐ **Look at the notes. Complete the sentences using *going to* and a verb.**

1 Nicola _isn't going to write_ letters on Monday.
  She _____ emails.

2 On Tuesday, Nicola _____
  shopping. She _____ her
  mum a present. She _____
  her dad a present.

3 On Wednesday, Nicola
  _____ a cake
  with her brother. She and her mother
  _____ a cake.

4 On Thursday, Nicola and Helen
  _____ to the café.
  They_____ to the library.

5 On Friday, Nicola _____ in.
  She _____ her homework.
  She _____ her friends.

6 She ____ _____ early on
  Saturday. She _____ late.

5 ⭐⭐⭐ **Write questions and answers.**

1 A: What/you/do/on Saturday morning?
  B: I/tidy my room.
  A: What are you going to do on Saturday
    morning?
  B: I'm going to tidy my room.

2 A: you/play football/this weekend?

B: No/not

A: _____

B: _____

3 A: your parents/buy you/a new computer?

B: Yes/

A: _____

B: _____

A: When/you/do/your homework?

B: I/do it after dinner

A: _____

B: _____

5 A: When/we/finish this project?

B: We/not/finish it. You/finish it. It's your homework!

A: _____

B: _____

6 A: Where/we/play our first concert?

B: We/play/it at the youth club. And we/play/ our second concert at the O2 Arena!!

A: _____

B: _____

Use your English: Invite, accept and refuse

6 ⭐ **Choose the correct words.**

A: ¹**Would** / **Do** you like to come to my birthday party?

B: When ²**it is** / **is it**?

A: It's on Saturday.

B: Yes, I'd love ³**to come** / **coming**. What time ⁴**does it start** / **it starts**?

A: At seven o'clock.

B: That ⁵**looks** / **sounds** great. Thanks.

A: Would you ⁶**like** / **want** to watch me play football on Saturday?

B: Saturday? I'm ⁷**frightened** / **afraid** I can't.

A: What about next week?

B: I'd like ⁸**it** / **to**, but I can't. I go to my grandparents' house every Saturday.

Grammar summary

Going to for future plans and intentions

Affirmative	Negative
I'm going to visit my aunt.	I'm not going to visit my aunt.
You're going to have a party.	You aren't going to have a party.
He's going to do more work.	He isn't going to do more work.
She's going to learn French.	She isn't going to learn French.
We're going to eat soon.	We aren't going to eat soon.
They're going to help us.	They aren't going to help us.

Questions	Short answers
Am I going to see you later?	Yes, you are./No, you aren't.
Are you going to have a party?	Yes, I am./No, I'm not.
Is he going to get a dog?	Yes, he is./No, he isn't.
Is she going to phone?	Yes, she is./No, she isn't.
Are we going to make a cake?	Yes, we are./No, we aren't.
Are they going to go by train?	Yes, they are./No, they aren't.

Note

Use

- We use *to be* + *going to* + infinitive to talk about future plans and intentions.
  I'm going to buy a new guitar.

Form

- To make negatives, we add *not (n't)* to the verb *to be*.
- In questions, the word order is (Question word) + *to be* + subject + *going to* + infinitive.
- In short responses we use the verb *to be*. We don't use *going to* or the main verb.
  Are you going to cook dinner? Yes, I am. NOT ~~Yes, I'm going to.~~

Common mistakes

~~I going to go to bed early tonight.~~ ✗
I'm going to go to bed early tonight. ✓
~~We are going to have a test tomorrow?~~ ✗
Are we going to have a test tomorrow? ✓

10 Language round-up

1 Rearrange the letters to complete the dialogue.

A: I think [1]*classical* (alslaccsi) music is [2]_____ (rnobgi). It's slow and old.

B: No, it isn't. It's really [3]_____ (genteritsni). Some pieces, like Beethoven's Fifth Symphony, are really [4]_____ (cniixegt).

A: Well, I prefer [5](ronyctu) _____ and (twsener) _____ music.

A: Most [6]_____ (asfumo) musicians aren't very [7]_____ (teednatl)

B: What do you mean?

A: I mean [8]_____ (ppo) stars and [9]_____ (par) singers. They don't play music, they just look good.

B: That's why I like TV talent shows. The people on them aren't just [10]_____ (gynuo) and [11]_____ (vttiertcaa). They're really good singers.

…/10

2 Complete the text with the correct form of the words in brackets.

The **CFI10** is a beautiful phone. It's the [1]*lightest* (light) of this month's new phones at only 80 grams. It costs £200 so it isn't [2]_____ (cheap) and it's [3]_____ (hard) to use than a lot of new phones, but it's great. The ELEGANT4 is [4]_____ (cheap) than the XP121Z. It's a little bit [5]_____ (heavy) than the CFI10 as well, but it's still [6]_____ (light) and [7]_____ (easy) to use. I like it. The KP008 is the [8]_____ (big) new phone. It's also the [9]_____ (heavy) and it's [10]_____ (difficult) to use than the other two. It is the [11]_____ (cheap) of the three phones, but isn't very good.

…/10

3 Complete the text with the words from the box.

- Are • to • better • near • ~~going~~ • best
- Is • more • aren't

Los Angeles band, 'Late for School' are [1] *going* to tour Europe next year. 'Late for School' are one of the [2]_____ new bands and they are going [3]_____ make a new CD. We asked their singer, Barry Hinks about life in the band.

Me: Barry, you're [4]_____ famous now than you were last year. Is your life very different?

Barry: No. We still live [5]_____ to our families.

Me: [6]_____ you going to change your style of music?

Barry: No. We [7]_____ going to start playing rap or folk!! Don't worry!

Me: [8]_____ Andy going to sing more songs on your new CD?

Barry: No. I'm a [9]_____ singer than him so I'm going to sing the songs!

…/8

4 Write questions and sentences.

1 What/you/do/next Saturday?

What are you going to do next Saturday?

2 Harry Potter/interesting/Twilight

_____

3 your mum/get/a new job next year?

_____

4 I/not/eat/any burgers next year

_____

5 famous/actor in the world/George Clooney

_____

6 My dad's phone/bad/phone in the world!

_____

7 Pizzas/nice/burgers

_____

…/12

🎧 15 **LISTEN AND CHECK YOUR SCORE**	
Total	…/40

10 Skills practice

SKILLS FOCUS: READING, LISTENING AND WRITING

Read

1 Read the texts and answer the questions.

1 Who didn't go shopping?   *Stella*

2 Who suggested a shop to go to?   _____

3 Who was late for the practice?   _____

4 Who got a red shirt?   _____

5 Who suggested going shopping?   _____

A __ Hi all, Enjoy Marrakesh! I'm going to stay in tomorrow and study. Can you get a cool shirt for me?
Thanks, Stella

B *1* Hi all, Our concert is in four days. What are we going to wear? Why don't we go shopping tomorrow evening? Do you want to come? Ashley

C __ Hi all, Thanks for yesterday, Cheryl. Sorry I was late. That was a fantastic practice. The concert is going to be amazing. Lucy

D __ Hi all, Great idea, Ashley. The best place to go is Marrakesh. Their clothes are beautiful. I can be there at 6 p.m. What about you? Lucy

E __ Hey, Stella, We bought you a red shirt. It's great. We're going to have a last practice tomorrow. It's going to be at Cheryl's house at 8 p.m. Don't be late. Ashley

2 Read the texts again and number them in the correct order.

Listen

3 🎧 **Listen and decide who is speaking.**

1 Stella and her sister   2 Ashley and Cheryl

4 🎧 **Listen again and answer the questions.**

1 How many people were at the concert?
   About fifty

2 Who was the happiest person in the band?
   _____

3 Who met a boy at the concert?
   _____

4 What time did they finish the concert?
   _____

5 How did they get home?
   _____

6 Which group do Lucy's parents think they are better than?
   _____

Write

5 Complete the email with the phrases from the box.

- in the end • because they were asleep
- at first • liked us • ~~on Saturday night~~
- with my sister

Hi Janey,
We played a great concert ¹ *on Saturday night*.
I was worried ²_____, but everything was OK ³_____. Cheryl sang really well. And Ashley is a great guitar player. All the people there really ⁴_____. We finished at ten o'clock and a lot of people wanted to talk to us. When I got home, I chatted ⁵_____ and then I went to bed. I didn't see my parents ⁶_____.
The next concert is in two weeks. I hope you can come.
Stella

Notes

Notes

Pearson Education Limited
Edinburgh Gate
Harlow
Essex CM20 2JE
England
and Associated Companies throughout the world.

www.english.com/livebeat

First published 2015

Eighth impression 2018

ISBN: 978-1-4479-5262-6

Set in Helvetica Neue LT Std 55 Roman 10/14pt

Printed by China (GCC)

Illustration Acknowledgements

(Key: b-bottom; c-centre; l-left; r-right; t-top)

David Banks p 46, 76; Jeremy Banx p 52; Adrian Barclay (Beehive Illustration) p 12, 13b, 16 (hot dog, chips, ice cream, tea), 45; Kathy Baxendale p 20, 21, 22, 24, 26, 32l, 63, 70, 72; Kevin Hopgood (Beehive Illustration) p 32r, 35, 58, 67; Joanna Kerr (New Division) p 16 (burger, crisps, cheese, chicken, hot chocolate, water), 36, 69; Pat Murray (Graham-Cameron Illustration) p 16r, 17; Anita Romeo (Advocate Illustration) p 13t, 44, 54; Eric Smith p 4, 7, 8, 14, 30, 40, 62, 64, 83; Tony Wilkins p 11

Photo Acknowledgements

The publisher would like to thank the following for their kind permission to reproduce their photographs:

(Key: b-bottom; c-centre; l-left; r-right; t-top)

Alamy Images: A.P.S. (UK) 11bl, Paula Solloway 43; **DK Images:** Diana Jarvis (c) Rough Guides 51tl; **Fotolia.com:** AM Design 71, ArtTo 27bl, Kevin Eaves 11cl, 75c, Laurent Hamels 29, David Hughes 51bl, janmadsenphotography 75t, jorgophotography 51tr, Łukasz Kurbiel 75b, Christopher Meder 27br, wajan 27t; **Getty Images:** Stephen Shugerman 31l; **Pearson Education Ltd:** Gareth Boden 36, Peter Evans 59, Matinee 38; **Photolibrary.com:** Hill Street Studios / Nicole Goddard 60; **Reuters:** Stephane Mahe 54; **Rex Features:** BEI / Jim Smeal 79r, MediaPunch 79c, Picture Perfect 31r, Startraks Photo 79l; **Shutterstock.com:** Dean Bertoncelj 57; **www.imagesource.com:** Corbis 11tl

All other images © Pearson Education

Cover images: *Front*: **Shutterstock.com:** Dmitry Lobanov

Every effort has been made to trace the copyright holders and we apologise in advance for any unintentional omissions. We would be pleased to insert the appropriate acknowledgement in any subsequent edition of this publication.